100
BAGGERS

100 BAGGERS

STOCKS THAT RETURN 100-TO-1 AND HOW TO FIND THEM

CHRISTOPHER MAYER

 Laissez Faire Books

In memory of Thomas W. Phelps,
author of the first book on 100-baggers

ISBN: 978-1-6212916-5-7

19 18 17 16 15   1 2 3 4 5 6 7

Published by Laissez Faire Books, 808 St. Paul Street, Baltimore, Maryland
www.lfb.org
www.agorafinancial.com

Cover and Layout Design: Andre Cawley

CONTENTS

CHAPTER 1:

INTRODUCING 100-BAGGERS

This book is about 100-baggers. These are stocks that return $100 for every $1 invested. That means a $10,000 investment turns into $1,000,000. In this book, I want to show you how you can find them.

I know, I know. It sounds like an outrageous quest with a wildly improbable chance of success, like setting out to draw a royal flush in poker. And I would probably have agreed with you not so long ago. But then I started to dig in and study these 100-baggers. Definite patterns emerged.

Let's set out what this book will do for you:

- You will learn the key characteristics of 100-baggers. There are only so many ways up the mountain, and we'll map out these paths in what follows.
- You will learn why anybody can do this. It is truly an everyman's approach. You don't need an MBA or a finance degree. Some basic financial concepts are all you'll need.
- I'll share with you a number of "crutches" or techniques that can help you get more out of your stocks and investing.
- The emphasis is always on the practical, and so there are many stories and anecdotes to help illustrate important points.

You should read this book if you want to get more out of your stocks. Even if you never get a 100-bagger, this book will help you turn up big winners and keep you away from sleepy stocks that go nowhere. If you like investing in utility stocks, with their limited upsides, then this book isn't for you.

This book will change the way you think about investing in stocks. You will never look at the problem in quite the same way again. I hope it will energize and excite you about what's possible.

Before I get to the specifics of how to find 100-baggers, let me give you some context that helps frame the whole effort.

The story of this book begins in 2011. That year, I read remarks investor Chuck Akre made at a conference held that same year. (Akre is a great investor, and we will meet him again in the last chapter.) The title of his talk was "An Investor's Odyssey: The Search for Outstanding Investments."

Here is part of what he said:

> In 1972, I read a book that was reviewed in *Barron's* and this book was called *100 to 1 in the Stock Market* by Thomas Phelps. He represented an analysis of investments gaining 100 times one's starting price. Phelps was a Boston investment manager of no particular reputation, as far as I know, but he certainly was on to something, which he outlined in this book. Reading the book really helped me focus on the issue of compounding capital. Also, from Boston, you all know Peter Lynch, who often spoke about ten-baggers. Here was Phelps talking about 100-baggers, so what's the deal? Well Phelps laid out a series of examples where an investor would in fact have made 100 times his money. Further he laid out some of the characteristics, which would compound these investments.

I had never heard of the book. And I've read all the investment classics and many obscure ones. So, I quickly got hold of a copy and began to read.

It became one of my favorite investing books. In December of that year, I sat down and wrote the following story for readers of my newsletter. It serves as an introduction to Phelps and the ideas we'll explore more in this book.

Every Problem Is an Investment Opportunity

"Every human problem is an investment opportunity if you can anticipate the solution," the old gentleman told me. "Except for thieves, who would buy locks?"

I just met this remarkable fellow, full of wisdom on investing, yet hardly known beyond a small group of fans. His name is Thomas Phelps, and he's had quite a career. He was the *Wall Street Journal*'s Washington bureau chief, an editor of *Barron's*, a partner at a brokerage firm, the head of the research department at a Fortune 500 company, and, finally, a partner at Scudder, Stevens & Clark (since bought out by Deutsche Bank). Phelps retired in Nantucket after a varied 42-year career in markets.

Along the way, Phelps figured out a few things about investing. He conducted a fascinating study on stocks that returned $100 for every $1 invested. Yes, 100 to 1. Phelps found hundreds of such stocks, bunches available in any single year, that you could have bought and enjoyed a 100-to-1 return on—if you had just held on.

This was the main thrust of our conversation: the key is not only finding them, but keeping them. His basic conclusion can be summed up in the phrase "buy right and hold on."

"Let's face it," he said: "a great deal of investing is on par with the instinct that makes a fish bite on an edible spinner because it is moving." Investors too bite on what's moving and can't sit on a stock that isn't going anywhere. They also lose patience with one that is moving against them. This causes them to make a lot of trades and never enjoy truly mammoth returns.

Investors crave activity, and Wall Street is built on it. The media feeds it all, making it seem as if important things happen every day. Hundreds of millions of shares change hands every session.

But investors need to distinguish between activity and results. "When I was a boy, a carpenter working for my father made this sage observation: 'A lot of shavings don't make a good workman.'" As you can see, Phelps is a man of folksy wisdom.

"Investors," Phelps continued, "have been so thoroughly sold on the nonsensical idea of measuring performance quarter by quarter—or even year by year—that many of them would hit the ceiling if an investment adviser or portfolio manager failed to get rid of a stock that acted badly for more than a year or two."

What investors should do is focus on the business, not on market prices. Phelps showed me financial histories of a long list of companies— earnings per share, returns on equity and the like. No stock prices. After one example, he asked, "Would a businessman seeing only those figures have been jumping in and out of the stock? I doubt it." But if they just sat on it, they'd be rich.

And this is the nub of it. Phelps is not a fan of selling good businesses.

He talked about how his friend Karl Pettit—an industrialist, inventor and investor—sold his shares of IBM stock many years ago to start his brokerage business. He sold them for a million bucks. That stake would eventually go on to be worth $2 billion—more than he ever made in his brokerage business.

Phelps told me the story of how he sold his Polaroid stock to pay a steep doctor's bill of $7,415 back in 1954. "Here is the confirmation of the sale," he said, and he keeps it as a reminder of his folly. Less than 20 years later, his Polaroid stock was worth $843,000. That's an expensive doctor's visit.

Phelps also stands against market timing. He told me about how he predicted various bear markets in his career. "Yet I would have been much better off if instead of correctly forecasting a bear market, I had focused my attention through the decline on finding stocks that would turn $10,000 into a million dollars."

Because of his bearishness, he missed opportunities that went on to deliver 100 to 1. "Bear market smoke gets in one's eyes," he said, and it blinds us to buying opportunities if we are too intent on market timing.

"He who lives by the sword shall perish by the sword," he added. "When experienced investors frown on gambling with price fluctuations in the stock market, it is not because they don't like money, but because both experience and history have convinced them that enduring fortunes are not built that way."

Phelps showed me a little table that reveals how much and for how long a stock must compound its value to multiply a hundredfold:

Return	Years to 100-bagger
14%	35 years
16.6%	30 years
20%	25 years
26%	20 years
36%	15 years

You'll note these are very long holding periods—especially in an age where the average holding period for stocks is measured in months—but that's the point. The greatest fortunes come from gritting your teeth and holding on.

You'll also see it's a fairly high hurdle to get to 100-bagger status. You need high growth for a long time. For example, Tractor Supply grew earnings at a rate of 23 percent per year and became a 100-bagger after just over 12 years. Later, we'll look at Monster Beverage, a stock that became a 100-bagger in just 10 years—a remarkable feat that required a 50 percent annual growth rate.

Phelps advises looking for new methods, new materials and new products—things that improve life, that solve problems and allow us to do things better, faster and cheaper. There is also an admirable ethical streak to Mr. Phelps's style, as he emphasized investing in companies that do something good for mankind. This requires looking beyond past figures.

"There is a Wall Street saying that a situation is better than a statistic," Phelps said. Relying only on published growth trends, profit margins and price-earnings ratios is not as important as understanding how a company could create value in the years ahead.

Phelps is quick to add he is not advocating blindly holding onto stocks. "My advice to buy right and hold on is intended to counter unproductive activity," he said, "not to recommend putting them away and forgetting them."

And so what if you don't get a hundredfold return? The point of Phelps's brilliant teaching method is to focus your attention on the power of compounding, to forget the day-to-day ripples of stock prices. After all, even if you catch part of a 100-bagger, the returns could fund a retirement.

It is an investment tragedy of a sort to think people have owned these stocks and not reaped those gains because they were trying to time the market or trade in and out. Sometimes stocks take a long time to get going. Phelps had plenty of examples of stocks that went nowhere (or down) for years but still delivered the big 100 to 1.

"One of the basic rules of investing is never, if you can help it, take an investment action for a noninvestment reason," Phelps advised. Don't sell just because the price moved up or down, or because you need to realize a capital gain to offset a loss. You should sell rarely, and only when it is clear you made an error. One can argue every sale is a confession of error, and the shorter the time you've held the stock, the greater the error in buying it—according to Phelps.

I love Mr. Phelps's ideas. They are hard to implement, I know. But some people have. He related the experiences of individuals, former clients and old associates, who got rich by buying right and holding on. Phelps wishes he had learned these insights when he was younger.

Now, I have a little confession to make about Mr. Phelps.

I didn't actually meet him. He's been dead since 1992, having reached the ripe old age of 90. Every quote above comes not from a conversation, but from his book *100 to 1 in the Stock Market: A Distinguished Security Analyst Tells How to Make More of Your Investment Opportunities*, published in 1972.

In 2011, I picked up a near-mint copy for $22. This forgotten book should be a classic. Do not let the implausibility of making 100 to 1 on your stocks distract you. The main idea is to know how such returns have happened and what investors need to do to get them. Aiming a little closer to that goal is bound to improve your results.

Phelps wrote as much: "Just a slight change in a golfer's grip and stance may improve his game, so a little more emphasis on buying for keeps, a little more determination not to be tempted to sell . . . may fatten your portfolio. In *Alice in Wonderland*, one had to run fast in order to stand still.

In the stock market, the evidence suggests, one who buys right must stand still in order to run fast." It is superb advice.

I recommend the book, needless to say, which is a pleasure to read and has plenty of good ideas, analogies and stories. For a long time, the book was out of print. But in January of 2015, Echo Point Books reissued the title, and you can buy it easily at Amazon. (Amazon is a 100-bagger we'll look at in chapter 5, by the way.)

Picking Up Where Phelps Left Off

Phelps's book was a study of 100-baggers from 1932 to 1971. It is not a study of *every* 100-bagger, because he properly limited his study to cut out the tiniest of stocks. (And I doubt even he had the resources to identify every 100-bagger.) It is also harder to come up with a definitive list than you'd think. There are complications in how you measure returns. (For example, do you measure stock prices annually, quarterly, daily, hourly? You get slightly different results each time, as some stocks may have only reached 100 times for a brief period.)

Even so, his book lists over 365 stocks. The latest 100-bagger started in 1967—that's a hundredfold return in just four years. But again, the cutoff is 1971.

I decided to update his study.

I started working with Stephen Jones (String Advisors) to create a database of every 100-bagger from 1962 through 2014—assuming you'd reinvested the dividends and also making allowances to cut the tiniest stocks. We looked for stocks that had a market cap of greater than $50 million, in today's dollars, prior to their hundredfold climb. This was a massive undertaking. My publisher spent more than $50,000 just to get the data.

My goal was and remains simple: I want to find what these stocks have in common. I want to learn how these spectacular returns came about, with an eye toward using those insights in today's market.

My new study would be an update of Phelps's work. I expected to reinforce many things Phelps wrote about. I also believed we'd uncover some new insights, since our computing horsepower vastly exceeds what was available to Phelps.

At the start, too, I wanted to write a new book around the study, to be called *100-Baggers*. I'd dedicate the book to the old man, Phelps.

So here we are.

An Everyman's Approach
to Huge Profits in Stocks

When I was younger, I had strong preconceptions about what great investing was all about. It was long-term, focused on the fundamentals and somehow a branch of Benjamin Graham and David Dodd's celebrated book called *Security Analysis*, a tree that yielded Warren Buffett and so many other great investors. If you weren't part of this intellectual tradition, you were just doing it wrong.

I'm not so doctrinaire anymore. I'll admit there are lots of ways to make money in markets, just as there are many different ways to make a really good pizza. Nonetheless, there is something to be said for a really good pizza that almost anyone can make with the right ingredients.

In the markets, you can find all kinds of crazy success stories, such as the improbable traders of *Market Wizards* fame—including Jim Rogers, Paul Tudor Jones and Michael Steinhardt—or the oddball dancer Nicolas Darvas, famous for his book *How I Made $2,000,000 in the Stock Market*, with its equally odd system. These never interested me, for many reasons, but one big reason is they struck me as freakish. The gains were enormous, but the process was not replicable—certainly not by the everyman. I had a hard time believing anyone using insights from such financial freaks could really get anywhere. More likely, I imagined, following such a path would lead to ruin.

But here is where Mr. Phelps is different. As you'll see in the next chapter, anyone can invest in a 100-bagger—and many ordinary people have. Anyone can find them—or find close-enough approximations. After all, who is going to complain if you only turn up a 50-bagger, or even a 10-bagger? Heck, most investors I know are delighted when they double their money in a few years.

Studying some of the great successes and the principles behind 100-baggers will help in the effort to find winning stocks today—not only 100-baggers. Before we get into that, which is the meat of the book, I want to discuss some elements of the study itself.

The Study: 365 Stocks
That Turned $10,000 into $1+ Million

Our study also turned up 365 stocks (by coincidence, the same number Phelps found in his study covering a different time period). This would be the main population of stocks I poked and prodded in the six months after we created the database.

I want to say a few words about what I set out to do—and what I don't want to do.

There are severe limitations or problems with a study like this. For one thing, I'm only looking at these extreme successes. There is hindsight bias, in that things can look obvious now. And there is survivorship bias, in that other companies may have looked similar at one point but failed to deliver a hundredfold gain. I am aware of these issues and others. They are hard to correct.

I had a statistician, a newsletter reader, kindly offer to help. I shared the 100-bagger data with him. He was aghast. He related his concerns using a little story. As he wrote to me,

> Let's say I am curious to find out what it is that makes basketball players so tall. So I take DNA and blood samples from the starting lineups of the NBA teams. There's something huge missing here, which is—all of the non-tall people!

And this is, of course, true—to an extent. I'm only looking at 100-baggers, not stocks that didn't make it. However, what I'll present in this book is not a set of statistical inferences, but a set of principles you can use to identify winners. If you've read Michael Lewis's *Moneyball*, which looks at the principles behind productive baseball players, you know this is a worthwhile exercise.

These principles I will share with you are undeniably true as points of logic, and you cannot get a 100-bagger without them. This will be clear to you by the end of the book.

We just have to be careful about what lessons we draw from any statistical analysis. So instead I have made a study more in the spirit of Phelps's original work. His work was more anecdotal than statistical. He relied heavily on common sense and basic truths. (This reminds me of *The Outsiders*, by William Thorndike, another important book, which we'll get to later.)

This study is useful in many ways, as I'll argue. But it is not meant as a scientific or statistical study. Investing is, arguably, more art than science, anyway. If investing well were all about statistics, then the best investors would be statisticians. And that is not the case.

We're looking for insights and wisdom, not hard laws and proofs.

So with that, let's get started.

CHAPTER 2:

ANYBODY CAN DO THIS: TRUE STORIES

Because it sounds utterly magical to invest $10,000 in a stock and walk away with $1 million some years later, Phelps emphasized how investing in 100-baggers was something achievable by anyone. One way he did this was to tell stories of real people who managed the feat.

I have many examples of my own.

When I started the 100-bagger project and began writing about it, I got a lot of email from readers who had netted a 100-bagger. People told me their stories. It is worth sharing a sampling of these early on because they help set the tone. Ordinary people can do this. You don't have to have an MBA or work at a hedge fund. And as you'll see, the lessons people drew from their experiences are exactly the ones this book will reinforce.

Here's one email:

As an active investor and trader for 30 years I have come to the realization that this 100-bagger approach and philosophy is the way one should approach a lifetime of investing. If one could only receive the proper level of mentoring as a young man, to commit oneself to this course. . . . If only I knew this when I started out, I would not only be wealthier, but my quality of life would have been vastly better through all those years.

I have had my share of home runs and plenty of disasters. I have spent countless days glued to the computer screen monitoring positions and trades. Over a career of investing and speculating the only real money that I held onto were [sic] in longer-term investments.

So my discovery in investing, and advice to younger ones who would endeavor to, [sic] is to study markets and invest in long term enterprises which have the potential to vastly outpace other companies and industries and stick with them as long as the theme is intact. Forget about the trading and use the time you would have spent monitoring the trade with your family.

It seems so simple, but few actually ever achieve it.

Here is a prime example of what I am talking about: Back in January 1992 I read the Barron's Roundtable and Felix Zulauf recommended Potash of Saskatchewan (POT) as a unique way to play the China growth story. . . . It all made sense to me so I took a modest position. The stock did quite well, I recall I bought it for $2/share. I held onto it for 3 years and got a 4–5 bagger out of it. I was pretty impressed with myself at my acute market acumen. It stalled out eventually and I sold it around 1996 as I got tired of it treading water. Now mind you the original premise never changed, it was always intact, yet I craved new action.

If I had held on until the blow off in 2007 I would have had my 100-bagger. If one had bought even earlier it was a 200+ bagger.

So the lesson is one needs to stick to the original theme and if it is intact just hold on. I believe your project is in fact a very achievable objective. One needs to isolate the common threads and place one's bets on the table after much research and conviction then hold on.

That's a good story, from someone who has won his wisdom the hard way. He hits on many important themes in this book. I'm going to have my 16-year-old son and my 13-year-old daughter read it, so they'll know it's not just Dad saying this stuff.

Here's another email:

I remember as a kid my dad used to grumble about my grandmother because she would complain that she couldn't see well and she had cataracts. He would say, well she doesn't seem to have any trouble reading the fine print in the WSJ when she is checking her Esso stock. That would have been around 1971 and somehow that is still in the recesses of my mind.

Now if one thinks this 100-bagger goal is unachievable, just consider as a young kid if I had just started accumulating ExxonMobil back then. It would not have taken a genius or much of a stock picker gene. Just buy the largest oil stock in the world that had been around for a hundred years. . . . Just put your blinders on and keep accumulating over a lifetime. No stress, no white knuckles since it has a very conservative balance sheet, no high wire act. So where [sic] would $1 back in 1971 in Esso be worth today? By my calculations $418 plus one would have been collecting a juicy dividend all those years.

Amazing, isn't it? Everybody has a story somewhat like these.

All right, one more, because these are so interesting:

In about 1969/1970, when a billboard in downtown Seattle read, "Will the Last Person Turn Out the Lights?" a friend of mine had just sold an apartment house in Seattle and netted about $100,000 after tax. His view was that things couldn't get any worse for Boeing so he bought 10,000 shares at $9.50/share. Within about 10 years or so he was getting annual cash dividends for almost as much as he had paid for the stock. This had to be a 100 plus bagger with all of the stock dividends and splits over the years. In 2002 I believe he still had not sold a share.

Key here is the idea that you must sit still. Think of all the reasons to sell Boeing since 1970: Inflation. Wars. Interest-rate worries. Economic fears. The list of reasons to sell is always long. But if you've done the job of picking right, you're better off holding on.

This reminds me of an anecdote by Chris Mittleman, an exceptional investor, published in one of his shareholder letters. An excerpt appeared in *Value Investor Insight*. Savor this:

> Imagine if a friend had introduced you to Warren Buffett in 1972 and told you, "I've made a fortune investing with this Buffett guy over the past ten years, you must invest with him." So you check out Warren Buffett and find that his investment vehicle, Berkshire Hathaway, had indeed been an outstanding performer, rising from about $8 in 1962 to $80 at the end of 1972. Impressed, you bought the stock at $80 on December 31, 1972. Three years later, on December 31, 1975, it was $38, a 53% drop over a period in which the S&P 500 was down only 14%. You might have dumped it in disgust at that point and never spoken to that friend again. Yet over the next year it rose from $38 to $94. By December 31, 1982 it was $775 and on its way to $223,615 today—a compounded annual return of 20.8% over the past 42 years.

I may print out the above and frame it.

So, anybody can do this. What you need to learn is how to buy right and then hold on. The latter sounds easy but is hard in practice. I'll offer a crutch in the next chapter. And later still, we'll deal with how to buy right.

CHAPTER 3:

THE COFFEE-CAN PORTFOLIO

"Have you ever heard of the coffee can portfolio?"

I was having lunch with Preston Athey, the outstanding investor behind T. Rowe Price's Small-Cap Value Fund, when he asked me this question.

I *had* heard of it, which I think surprised him a little because I was only 12 years old when the idea came out, and it is not a mainstream idea. I knew all about it, though, because the coffee-can portfolio is one of those classic ideas that aficionados of finance don't forget.

I want to tell you about the coffee-can portfolio. It is an excellent crutch to 100-baggerdom. It will help you "hold on."

It all began with Robert Kirby, then a portfolio manager at Capital Group, one of the world's largest investment-management firms. He first wrote about the coffee-can idea in the fall of 1984 in the *Journal of Portfolio Management*. "The coffee can portfolio concept harkens back to the Old West, when people put their valuable possessions in a coffee can and kept it under the mattress," Kirby wrote. "The success of the program depended entirely on the wisdom and foresight used to select the objects to be placed in the coffee can to begin with."

The idea is simple: you find the best stocks you can and let them sit for 10 years. You incur practically no costs with such a portfolio. And it is certainly easy to manage. The biggest benefit, though, is a bit more subtle and meaningful. It works because it keeps your worst instincts from hurting you. In his paper, Kirby told the story about how his idea came about.

"The coffee can idea first occurred to me in the 1950s," Kirby wrote. Back then, he worked for a big firm that counseled individuals on their investments. He had a client he worked with for 10 years whose husband died suddenly. She inherited his stock portfolio, which she moved to Kirby's care. Looking at the portfolio, Kirby wrote,

> I was amused to find that [her husband] had been secretly piggybacking our recommendations for his wife's portfolio. Then I looked at the size of the estate. I was also shocked. The husband had applied a small twist of his own to our advice: He paid no attention whatsoever to the sale recommendations. He simply put about $5,000 in every purchase recommendation. Then he would toss the certificate in his safe-deposit box and forget it.

In doing this, a wonderful thing happened. Yes, it meant his portfolio had a number of broken stocks that came to be worth $2,000 or so. Small positions. But he also had a few holdings that ended up worth $100,000 each. The kicker, though, was this: he had one jumbo position of $800,000 that alone was bigger than the total value of his wife's portfolio. As Kirby wrote, "[It] came from a small commitment in a company called Haloid; this later turned out to be a zillion shares of Xerox."

That is an inspiring tale, a triumph of lethargy and sloth. It shows clearly how the coffee-can portfolio is designed to protect you against yourself—the obsession with checking stock prices, the frenetic buying and selling, the hand-wringing over the economy and bad news. It forces you to extend your time horizon. You don't put anything in your coffee can you don't think is a good 10-year bet.

Poor Kirby had been diligently managing the wife's account—keeping up with earnings reports, trimming stocks and adding new positions.

All the while, he would have been better off if he'd followed the idler's creed and just stuck with his initial ideas.

Why don't more people hold on?

Phelps wrote that investors have been conditioned to measure stock-price performance based on quarterly or annual earnings but not on business performance. One memorable example he uses (among many) is Pfizer, whose stock lost ground from 1946 to 1949 and again from 1951 to 1956. "Performance-minded clients would have chewed the ears off an investment adviser who let them get caught with such a dog," Phelps wrote. But investors who held on from 1942 to 1972 made 141 times their money.

Phelps showed that if you just looked at the annual financial figures for Pfizer—ignoring the news, the stock market, economic forecasts and all the rest—you would never have sold the stock. It was profitable throughout, generating good returns on equity, with earnings climbing fitfully but ever higher.

Pfizer was a good coffee-can stock.

An Extreme Coffee-Can Portfolio

Few things are harder to put up with than the annoyance of a good example.

— Mark Twain, *Pudd'nhead Wilson*

Just to give you an extreme example of this sort of thing, imagine sitting still for 80 years.

There is a portfolio that makes the coffee-can portfolio look impatient: the Voya Corporate Leaders Trust Fund. It was the subject of a story written for Reuters by Ross Kerber. The headline was "Buy-and-Hold Fund Prospers with No New Bets in 80 Years."

Now, I know you have no interest in holding stocks for 80 years. I don't, either. In fact, 10 years is pushing it. I know that. Still, that doesn't mean we can't learn something from the story.

Here's Kerber:

The Voya Corporate Leaders Trust Fund, now run by a unit of
Voya Financial Inc bought equal amounts of stock in 30 major US
corporations in 1935 and hasn't picked a new stock since.

Talk about set it and forget it!

What's so interesting is the story the portfolio tells. It still has some
of the same names it had in 1935: DuPont, General Electric, Proctor &
Gamble and Union Pacific.

But it also has positions that came about through mergers and/or
spinoffs. For example, it owns Berkshire Hathaway via an original position
in the Atchison, Topeka and Santa Fe Railway. It has CBS via a stake in Westinghouse Electric. It owns Honeywell through a stake in Allied Chemical.

It has shares in Foot Locker because that's where a 1935 position in F.
W. Woolworth wound up. It owns ExxonMobil and Chevron, thanks to an
investment in Rockefeller's Standard Oil.

There are only 21 names left, as some have gone on to the great big
board in the sky, such as American Can and the Pennsylvania Railroad Co.

Remarkably, the fund has beaten 98 percent of its peers over the last
five- and ten-year periods. Wrote Kerber,

Over the five year period ended Feb. 24 [2015] the fund returned
an average of 17.32 percent a year, including fees, 1.03 percentage
point better than the S&P 500, said Morningstar. For the 10 years
ended Feb. 24 the fund returned an average of 9.40 percent a year,
including fees, 1.32 percentage point better than the S&P 500.

In fact, it's beaten the S&P 500 for 40 years. The fund's website doesn't
go back any further than that, though I wonder what its performance has
been like since inception.

It is a low-cost fund, with a fee of just 52 basis points, or 0.52 percent.
(Most funds' fees are triple that.) And there are few capital gains taxes to
pay, thanks to low turnover. (The fund still has to buy and sell to meet
redemptions and invest new money.)

All in all, a remarkable little story about the power of sitting tight in a portfolio of carefully chosen stocks based on a sensible investment strategy.

The fund's original sponsor was Corporate Leaders of America. Today, after a series of deals, it's under Voya's umbrella. The original fund had a simple mandate, as described in a brochure on the fund's history:

> The founders of the Trust bought equal shares of 30 leading companies in 1935 and decreed they could never be sold. The only exception was companies that went bankrupt, merged or spun off.

You don't find them making any more funds like this. But back in the early days of the mutual fund industry, most funds looked more like it than not.

The first open-ended mutual fund in America—and in the world— was the Massachusetts Investors Trust, established in 1924.

(An aside: Open-ended means you could buy and sell shares of the fund at a price that matched the value of its portfolio. Before MIT came along, funds were closed-end. This meant prices might not match the underlying value of the portfolio. Disclosures were poor. And as you can imagine, sponsors often manipulated prices to their advantage.)

MIT was something new under the sun. It promised transparency and fairness. It promised low-cost professional management for the small investor. It had a sensible and conservative investment policy with a focus on large dividend-paying stocks. MIT would not trade these stocks, but aim to buy and hold.

As the late great professor Louis Lowenstein of Columbia University wrote,

> The transparency and flexibility, and the security and comfort thus offered to small investors, made MIT a uniquely American contribution to finance. . . . Good ideas usually have simple beginnings: it's the very simplicity of the concept that makes them ultimately successful. This one was brilliant.

Lowenstein told MIT's story well in his book *The Investor's Dilemma*, which I highly recommend to anyone who invests in mutual funds.

(Lowenstein is also the author of my two favorite books on corporate finance: *Sense & Nonsense in Corporate Finance* and *What's Wrong with Wall Street.*)

Like Voya, MIT held onto stocks for a long time. In 1949, the average holding period was 27 years. (Note this is an implied holding period based on the fund's turnover. In 1949, the fund was not yet 27 years old.) And it attracted like-minded investors. Redemptions were less than 3 percent per year. The fee was only 40 basis points (or 0.4 percent). By 1960, the fee would drop to just 19 basis points.

But unlike Voya, this tale has a sad ending. MIT's story also illustrates another old truism: Wall Street often turns good ideas into bad ones. It would soon corrupt the simple, brilliant idea of the open-ended mutual fund and turn it into just another moneymaker for Wall Street.

The problem with MIT from Wall Street's perspective is that nobody could make any money off it—except the investors in the fund. So, somehow, somebody convinced MIT to take on an external manager in 1969. Before that, MIT had its own managers in-house. This was the beginning of the end.

With an external manager, the fee started to go up. By 1969, the fee was up 36-fold while assets under management were up just 7-fold. The external manager also managed the fund more aggressively and traded more frequently. A sad decline set in. By 2004, Blackrock bought the fund and merged it with others. MIT was no more.

The typical fund these days charges a lot, trades way too much and trails the market badly. Lowenstein wrote in his book that the average fund has 160 stocks and turns them over every year. That's not investing. But Wall Street makes money.

The establishment doesn't want you to just sit on carefully chosen stocks. It wants to charge you fees. It wants to sell you stuff.

This brings us back again to the Voya fund. MIT's tale makes it seem all the more incredible the Voya fund lasted as long as it has with its initial mission intact. It's a special fund, a piece of Americana.

Okay, so maybe you don't hold stocks for 80 years. And maybe even my coffee-can approach—with its 10-year holding period—is still too long-term for you.

But there is surely some young person in your life whom you can share the wisdom of long-term investing with. Tell them about the coffee-can idea. Tell them the story of the Voya fund. Make them wise to the ways of Wall Street.

Regarding these extreme holding periods, a reader wrote to me the following:

So my thoughts are that this coffee can is a nice way to leave a legacy for my children and grandchildren. I am 66 years old and 35-year investments (I know that you consider coffee can 10 years but it seems to be that the longer you can go the better it gets) are probably not a good idea now. I was intrigued by the fund that invested in a basket of stocks in 1935 and never touched it again. I am not sure how one would do this now but it is an approach that saves us from ourselves.

The question: How would you go about identifying companies for a 35-year coffee can? When I looked at your list of the best performers almost all of them were over 25 year or greater returns. If I had tried to pick long-term investments in 1970 my guess is that I would have invested in stocks like Sears, GE, US Steel, Westinghouse, Exxon and such members of the DOW. Some would have been ok, such as GE and Exxon but there would have been no investments in Wal-Mart, Apple, Microsoft, etc. and some would have been bad. Would we be better off buying shares of wise investors such as Buffett and sitting on those? The downside is that none of the current wise guys will be around in 35 years either.

The questions raised are difficult to answer, especially now, because things change so quickly. For example, take a look at the average lifespan of a firm in the S&P 500 index. It is now less than 20 years. See the chart on the next page.

The average lifespan was 61 years in 1958. So things have changed a great deal. At the current rate, Innosight estimates, 75 percent of the current S&P will be replaced by 2027. Leaving the S&P 500 doesn't mean the death of the firm. But unless there is a buyout, S&P usually kicks you out only when you are in trouble—for example, Circuit City, the New York Times, Kodak or Bear Stearns. Or they kick you out when you get too small—which is another way of saying you underperformed. (Although dropped stocks tend to outperform in the first year after being dropped, excluding those bought out.)

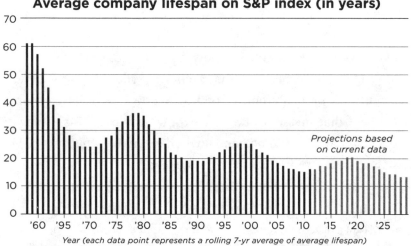

Average company lifespan on S&P index (in years)

Year (each data point represents a rolling 7-yr average of average lifespan)

I'll show you one more chart to make a point. Here is the average asset life of US firms, by sector, as of 2013:

	Asset Life
Information Technology	6.6
Healthcare	11.4
Consumer Discretionary	12.4
Consumer Staples	15.1
Industrials	15.4
Telecommunication Services	16.1
Energy	17.6
Materials	18.6
Utilities	29.4

This table comes from a report by Michael Mauboussin published in 2014 and titled "A Long Look at Short-Termism." Mauboussin is an investment strategist and author of several well-regarded books and research papers. He wrote, "The average asset life of companies in the US is shortening." And more and more firms are in shorter-asset-life industries. Mauboussin concluded,

> Shorter asset lives suggest shorter time horizons over which managers should invest, a reasonable reflection of the business world. Executives of many technology companies, for example, can't plan for decades in the way a utility company can because the rate of change is simply too fast.

So, 35 years is probably too long a horizon to plan over. This creates some tension with the 100-bagger idea. There is a tension between holding on and the potentially destructive effect of time. Nothing lasts forever.

We'll look at what kinds of companies to focus on in the next chapter. But we're not yet done exploring the coffee-can idea.

The Biggest Hurdle to Making 100 Times Your Money

The reason I spend a lot of time here at the beginning showing you the power of long-term investing is because it's really important. The biggest hurdle to making 100 times your money in a stock—or even just tripling it—may be the ability to stomach the ups and downs and hold on.

The coffee-can is a foolproof way to inoculate yourself against those sickening ups and downs.

And I'm sure you've seen some big moves in the overall market in your time. The urge to grab a quick gain or let go of a "loser" is strong. We're like the little kids in those famous experiments who can't resist eating the marshmallow in front of them even when promised two if they wait five minutes.

Even the best investors have their share of stories of when they couldn't wait. One of the best is from Warren Buffett. A reader and friend of mine sent me the following example, from Buffett's 1995 letter to Berkshire Hathaway shareholders:

> I first became interested in Disney in 1966, when its market valuation was less than $90 million, even though the company had

earned around $21 million pretax in 1965 and was sitting with more cash than debt. At Disneyland, the $17 million Pirates of the Caribbean ride would soon open. Imagine my excitement—a company selling at only five times rides!

Duly impressed, Buffett Partnership Ltd. bought a significant amount of Disney stock at a split-adjusted price of 31 cents per share. That decision may appear brilliant, given that the stock now sells for $66. But your Chairman was up to the task of nullifying it: In 1967 I sold out at 48 cents per share.

He made a 55 percent gain, but what a costly sale that was!

The problem isn't only that we're impatient. It's that the ride is not often easy. This reminds me of a story from 2012 by fund manager Dan Oliver at Myrmikan Capital. He pointed out that Apple from its IPO in 1980 through 2012 was a 225-bagger.

But . . .

Those who held on had to suffer through a peak-to-trough loss of 80 percent—twice! The big move from 2008 came after a 60 percent drawdown. And there were several 40 percent drops. Many big winners suffered similar awful losses along the way.

Author Barry Ritholtz in a column in the *Washington Post* had many more examples. Netflix, which has been a 60-bagger since 2002, lost 25 percent of its value in a single day—four times! On its worst day, it fell 41 percent. And there was a four-month stretch where it dropped 80 percent.

And yet, you can't just hold onto everything. Lots of big winners have gone completely bust. Ritholtz mentioned a few: Lehman Brothers, WorldCom, Lucent and JDS Uniphase. I'm sure we could come up with more.

So it takes patience, some savvy stock picking and—as with most things in life—some luck. (People who held onto Apple for the whole ride had no way of knowing about the iPod or iPhone or iPad. These things didn't exist for decades during Apple's run.)

This is where the idea of a coffee-can portfolio can help. You don't have to put all of your money in a coffee-can portfolio. You just take a portion you know you won't need for 10 years. I bet the final results will exceed those from anything else you do.

A Coffee-Can for the Apocalypse

You might think a coffee-can portfolio depends on an optimistic view, à la the one Warren Buffett expressed in his 2015 annual letter.

It doesn't. You can have quite a dim view of the world, and still I'd recommend you build a coffee-can portfolio. Below, I'll explain why.

But first, a bit on Buffett's optimism.

I read his annual letter. I also read a lot of commentary on the letter. One of the more interesting criticisms comes from SNL Financial columnist Ada Lee. She writes,

> The greatest flaw in the letter is the same as last year's greatest flaw; Buffett is given to expressing bullishness on America's prospects in a way that seems almost designed to instill precisely the sort of complacency that poses the greatest risk to that bullish view.

In the letter, Buffett writes how he "always considered a 'bet' on ever-rising US prosperity to be very close to a sure thing. Indeed, who has ever benefited during the past 238 years by betting against America?"

To that, Lee has a good response:

> Nobody. Unfortunately, that sort of statement is completely true right up to the day it is completely false. One might have said the same thing about Athens right up to the start of the Peloponnesian War, or Rome through the rule of Augustus, or even the Soviet Union up until around 1980, after which a great many people benefitted immeasurably by betting against those states.

So that sets the table for thinking about a future that might not be quite as prosperous. What do past calamities tell us about preserving wealth?

Many have tried to answer it. The first guy I thought of was the late Barton Biggs. He was a longtime strategist at Morgan Stanley and then a hedge fund manager and author. (*Hedgehogging* is his best book and worth reading.)

But Biggs was something of a catastrophist. History's periods of great wealth destruction, where the Four Horsemen of the Apocalypse ran wild, transfixed him. He worried about disasters happening again. He asked the timeless question "How to do you preserve wealth in times when the Four Horsemen are on the loose?"

It was one of the two questions that, in his own words, "long obsessed" him. The other was whether the stock market was wise in its judgments or merely a "foolish consensus of crowds."

One of his books, *Wealth, War and Wisdom*, dealt explicitly with these questions through the lens of World War II history, a hobby interest of his.

On the wisdom of crowds, Biggs found that the stock markets of the world showed "surprisingly good intuitions at the epic turning points. As the old saying goes, when coming events cast their shadows, they often fall on the NYSE."

He wrote how

- "the British stock market bottomed . . . in 1940 just before the Battle of Britain";
- "the US market turned forever in late May 1942 around the epic Battle of Midway"; and
- the German market "peaked at the high-water mark of the German attack on Russia just before the advance German patrols actually saw the spires of Moscow in early December 1941."

"Those were the three great momentum changes of World War II," he wrote, "although at the time, no one except the stock markets recognized them as such."

I must admit those are amazing intuitions. It's easy to write off the market as nutty when it doesn't agree with you, but Biggs made the case that the collective judgment of the market can be wiser than we allow. In any event, this is tangential to what I consider the meaty second question.

The second question dealt with how to preserve wealth when the Four Horsemen are on the loose. Biggs went through a lot of WWII-era carnage to find answers. You'll find such chapter headings and subheads as "Preserving Wealth in a Time of Cholera," "The Plunder of Land in Poland," "The Seizure of Estates in Hungary," "The Theft of Land and Valuables in Czechoslovakia" and "Rape and Robbery by the Red Army."

And yet, after all that, even the catastrophist Biggs recommended putting 75 percent of your wealth in stocks.

This is partly because his own understanding of the history of catastrophes validated such a move—stocks were still often the best way to preserve purchasing power over a period of years, even in devastated Germany. But it is also because he understood the best shot you have at growing your wealth is to own stuff. You want to be an owner.

If you own stocks, you are part owner in a real business—with real people trying to figure things out and with real assets and real profits. Ownership of assets is your best long-term protection against calamity.

But what to do with the other 25 percent?

Biggs recommended a much smaller part of your wealth go toward a ranch or family farm. He advocated a safe haven, well stocked with seed, fertilizer, canned food, wine, medicines, clothes and so on.

This survivalist stuff is not my main idea. I just want to make the point that in real collapse, your portfolio will probably be among the least of your worries. But at least in a calamity like WWII, stocks were your best bet.

So, let's pull this back to the coffee-can idea and think about a coffee can for catastrophists.

First, your coffee can doesn't have to include stocks. You could, if you were so inclined, stuff your coffee can with gold. I wouldn't do that, but the point is the coffee-can idea is not an expression of Buffett-like optimism on America. You could put whatever you want in your coffee can.

The essence of the coffee-can idea is really that it's a way to protect you against yourself—from the emotions and volatility that make you buy or sell at the wrong times. Bullishness or bearishness doesn't enter into it.

If you are a bear and abstain from using a coffee can, you're basically saying you'll make a series of better short-term decisions over the next 10 years than you would if you just sat on your best ideas today. That seems unlikely, given all the research that shows how most investors trade too much and how it hurts their returns.

Put another way, the theory behind the coffee can says your series of shorter-term decisions is likely to be worse than one decision today. It might not turn out that way, but it is independent of whether you think the world will be less prosperous in 10 years.

If the world is worse off in 10 years, that will affect all strategies. It's not as if you can say, "Well, I think the United States is going to be the next Argentina, and hence I won't use the coffee can." The conclusion does not follow from the premise. You still have to decide what to do.

And as I've said before, you don't have to put all of your wealth in a coffee can. I've told people they only need to put a part of their money in a coffee can. It doesn't have to be the only approach you use, but it can be one of several.

In summary, don't let the fear of apocalypse keep you from a building a coffee-can portfolio.

A Footnote to the Coffee-Can Portfolio

I love the coffee-can concept. And one of the reasons is that anyone can use it. It melds perfectly with the idea of 100-baggers, because if you truly want 100-baggers, you need to give stocks some time. We'll cover this more later, but since 1962, there have only been 20—out of the 365 included in my study—that did so inside of 10 years.

But if you do give your stocks time to marinate, the results can be mind-blowing. And when you think about it, it is not really that hard to simply not sell. I have to share a few more stories from real people who resisted selling and accumulated small fortunes.

Here is a coffee can story for you. My brother and I were heirs to 2000 shares each of Praxair in 1998. I believe it was worth about $34,000 at the time. I did not reinvest the dividends (wish I had) but adjusted the "purchase" price by the amount of the dividends received each year.

I stopped doing the adjusting when the imputed price had dropped to $1.20 per share (didn't want it to go below zero). The price is now about $126, so this effectively meets your criterion of a 100-fold increase, even if the stock price itself has not gone up 100-fold. The stock actually was probably purchased by my Dad at a price close to the $1 mark . . . The total value is now over a quarter million.

I find these stories inspiring. I also like the homespun quality of the stories. The above letter writer is not a hotshot hedge fund manager. He's just a normal guy who held onto a stock.

Here's another one:

I am very interested in the coffee can scenario because my personal experience is that this is the only way I really make money. I have two hits and one huge miss over the years that would have been coffee can type investments.

My first hit was a 200 share investment in a small startup called Micros Systems. I paid $1.30 for the shares. It grew and split several times since I bought it in 1981 or 82 (something like that) and was purchased last year by a large tech firm. I received $54,000 for my stock.

The second was $3,500 in General Electric stock. . . . I was an employee for 3 years and invested through payroll withholding which GE matched. That investment grew to over $125,000. . . . The bottom line was buying and leaving it alone.

The one huge miss was Telefonos de Mexico. I bought 600 shares of this in 82 and sold it when it doubled. Boy was that a mistake. If I had left it alone, well. . . .

You would think this strategy would have greater appeal than it does. After all, how many people want to spend a large part of their time following ticker symbols, anxiously watching blinking lights on a screen and following the ups and downs of the market?

It seems to me a better existence to instead know what you own and then really own it, as you would a rental property. Then you go about your life without all the baggage and worry that comes from sweating over the day-to-day or month-to-month value of your portfolio.

Here's a story that includes a good point on the 100-bagger theme:

Re: 100 baggers, I thought you might be interested in my one experience with a 100-bagger. In 1987, I invested equal amounts in 10 high-tech or biotech companies that had fabulous stories, and that if they could actually get their products or software to market would be huge winners. Well, I tried to be somewhat smart in picking them, but 9 of the 10 went completely under, and in a not-very-long time either. There were myriad problems, but most had to do with being undercapitalized. The 10th one, a startup named Amgen, hit it, and not only made up for the other 9 total losses but returned 800 times my total investment before I had to sell it to send my kids to college in '94. Wish I still had it, heh.

Two takeaways for me here: you must pick a compelling story (or leader or country or . . .) and you must use money you can afford to lose because you must be willing to risk it all. All of it.

This is a good point and bears repeating. With a coffee can, you are allowing yourself to potentially lose everything on a single position. But the idea is that the returns on the overall coffee-can portfolio more than make up for any such disasters.

I don't recommend taking on start-up risks in your coffee can. I would stick with more established companies with long runways of growth ahead and the ability to keep compounding capital at a high rate.

Now that you know to hold on, let's turn to what kind of stocks you want to put in it. Let's look at those 100-baggers.

CHAPTER 4:

STUDIES OF 100-BAGGERS

There have been a number of prior studies of 100-baggers, besides Phelps's excellent book. I don't know whether I've found them all, but I've found a few. In at least a pair of them, Phelps was an inspiration.

There are, of course, countless studies on stocks that outperform. But here I'm focusing specifically on the 100-bagger phenomenon, or close likenesses.

I want to highlight some of these, because they lay more groundwork for what follows. And many of the principles uncovered here are ones I'll emphasize later. There are only so many paths to 100-baggerdom, and these trailblazers—including Phelps himself—have helped map out the territory.

Tony's 100-Baggers

A fellow named Tony at TS Analysis published one informal 15-page study called "An Analysis of 100-Baggers." You can find it free online. "I am not an investment adviser or financial analyst"—Tony writes—"just a guy who likes to analyze stocks."

He looked at 19 such 100-baggers. He drew four conclusions, which I excerpt below:

- The most powerful stock moves tended to be during extended periods of growing earnings accompanied by an expansion of the P/E ratio.
- These periods of P/E expansion often seem to coincide with periods of accelerating earnings growth.
- Some of the most attractive opportunities occur in beaten-down, forgotten stocks, which perhaps after years of losses are returning to profitability.
- During such periods of rapid share price appreciation, stock prices can reach lofty P/E ratios. This shouldn't necessarily deter one from continuing to hold the stock.

Hansen Natural (now Monster Beverage) is a classic illustration of these points.

Tony showed how earnings growth rates went from negative in 2001 to 0 percent in 2002. From there, earnings increased on a quarterly basis by 20 percent, 40 percent and then 100 percent. In 2004, quarterly earnings growth accelerated to 120 percent, and then 150 percent, 170 percent and finally 220 percent by the fourth quarter.

Meanwhile, the price–earnings ratio also ramped up. In 2001, earnings were just 4 cents per share and the stock had a P/E of 10. By 2006, earnings were about $1 per share and the P/E was 50.

Think about that. Earnings went up 25-fold, but thanks to the market putting a bigger multiple on those earnings, the stock went up 125-fold. (We'll look at Monster Beverage in more detail in the next chapter.)

Growth, growth and more growth are what power these big movers.

There was a good case study of a 100-bagger recently posted on the Microcap Club's website by Chip Maloney. This is worth spending a little time on and illustrates Tony's principles. Maloney reviewed MTY Foods, which is a Canadian franchisor of quick-service restaurants such as Thai Express, Extreme Pita and TCBY.

In 2003, MTY Foods had a $5 million market cap. Every dollar invested in MTY Foods then was worth $100 by 2013. The question Maloney asks is the question I've asked myself many times in writing this book. Essentially, how did this 100-bagger become a 100-bagger?

In this case, the story begins with Stanley Ma, who became president of the company in 2003. MTY had a fast-food franchising business. And Ma "was the entrepreneur who started the company's very first restaurant concept Tiki Ming—Chinese Cuisine in 1987 as a recent immigrant to Canada."

What's most remarkable about this is Ma bought 20 percent of the company when he became president. Altogether, he owned 29 percent of the firm. As an owner-operator, he had every incentive to make the stock work.

Maloney goes through a number of reasons why MTY was successful. It starts with Ma. But it was a remarkable opportunity on many other levels as well. Here are a few attributes I've chosen from Maloney's more extensive list:

- Stock traded for two times forward earnings (cheap!).
- Business was a cash cow with 70 percent gross margins.
- Long runway—MTY was just a tiny fraction of the fast-food industry.

Ma created new restaurant concepts (5, all told) and bought others (19, eventually). The names and details are not important. What's important is that these new and acquired concepts allowed MTY to increase its number of locations. These businesses generated high profits. So, taking those profits and reinvesting them created a flywheel of rapidly growing revenues and earnings. You can see this clearly in the table on the next page, "MTY's path to coveted 100-bagger status."

Maloney makes an interesting observation here:

Earnings per share grew by a factor of 12.4x. But if the company only grew earnings by 12.4x, how did the stock grow 100x? The answer lies in the price to earnings (P/E) multiple expansion. Investors in MTY went from paying roughly 3.5x earnings when it was left for dead in 2003 to a more optimistic 26x earnings in 2013.

MTY's path to coveted 100-bagger status

	Revenues (mill)	EPS	# of locations	Share Price
2003	$11.50	$0.10	260	$0.34
2004	$15.50	$0.19	420	$2.50
2005	$18.62	$0.27	527	$3.85
2006	$22.40	$0.33	784	$6.40
2007	$30.53	$0.48	825	$12.63
2008	$34.24	$0.52	1023	$7.34
2009	$51.50	$0.64	1570	$9.15
2010	$66.90	$0.81	1727	$14.40
2011	$78.50	$0.84	2263	$15.30
2012	$96.20	$1.15	2199	$22.25
2013	$101.40	$1.34	2590	$34.34
Growth	7.8x	12.4x	9x	100x

So, again, you need huge growth in earnings. But the combination of rising earnings and a higher multiple on those earnings is really what drives explosive returns over the long-term. And in this case, long-term wasn't really all that long—just 10 years.

I call these two factors—growth in earnings and a higher multiple on those earnings—the "twin engines" of 100-baggers. We will come to this point again.

Microcaps and 100-Baggers

As usually defined, a microcap is a stock with a market cap of less than $300 million.

Microcaps actually dominate the market in terms of number of stocks. There are about 16,000 publicly traded stocks in the United States. About 7,360 are under $500 million. From there, here's how the market caps break down, from Dave Gentry's book *Microcap Superstars*:

- 7,360 under $500 million
- 6,622 under $250 million
- 5,713 under $100 million
- 5,053 under $50 million

That means at least 40 percent of the companies in the market are microcaps. This is a vast area to explore. And somewhere in this mix are tomorrow's big companies. I'm stating the obvious, but many big companies started out small. Gentry lists among these the following:

- Starbucks began in 1971 in Seattle as a small store sell ing coffee beans and today is worth $76 billion in the stock market.

- Apple began in 1976 in a garage with a $10,000 invest ment and today is worth $766 billion.

- Subway began as a single sandwich shop in Bridgeport, CT, and a $1,000 investment—and today generates over $9 billion in sales in over 35,000 locations.

You get the idea. Small companies can grow to 10 times or 20 times and still be small. They can even become 100-baggers. Apple today, by contrast, has a $766 billion market cap. We can safely assume it won't go up 10 times or 20 times and certainly not a hundredfold.

The Alchemy behind 100-Baggers

My focus is on the US market, but I've wondered what such a study might look like in other markets.

Fortunately, one such study exists. A firm called Motilal Oswal put together a study of 100-baggers in India. Published in December 2014, the authors of the report also found their inspiration in Phelps's work and dedicated their report to him.

It's a fine report, and there is much wisdom in it. "Very few investors even conceptualize their equity investment multiplying 100 times," they wrote. "Even fewer actually experience a 100-fold rise in the price of their stock(s). This is because such 100-fold rises may take longer than three, five or even 10 years' time. And holding onto stocks beyond that period requires patience."

Indeed it does, as you well know by now. Nearby is a chart that neatly plots the returns required, and the years needed, to reach 100-bagger status.

Years it takes for 100x at different rates

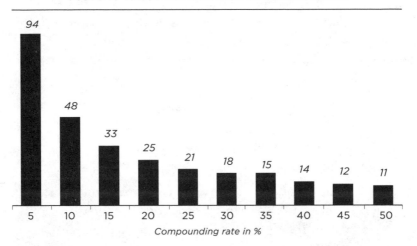

Compounding rate in %

You don't have to hold onto a stock for 20 years to get a 100-bagger. But the idea is to show you the power of long-term compounding. To harness that power takes some time.

The Oswal study found 47 enduring 100-baggers in India over the past 20 years. It excluded fleeting bubble-like stocks. What's shocking is that the Indian stock market as a whole is a 100-bagger relative to 1979. "The BSE Sensex has a base of 100 for the year 1979," the Oswal report noted. "The Sensex first touched 10,000 in February 2006." That's a 100-bagger in 27 years, or 19 percent annually. As I write, the Sensex is at 27,000.

What I find most interesting are Oswal's conclusions.

After all, the aim here is to apply what we learn from the study to help us find 100-baggers today. Based on my work (and Phelps's), it's easy to agree with Oswal when he wrote the single most important factor "is GROWTH in all its dimensions—sales, margin and valuation."

Most 100-baggers had huge growth curves in these areas. Studying 100-baggers, then, comes down to studying growth: How it happens. And how it endures—as it must to reach the heights of 100-baggerdom. As the chart shows, a 21 percent annual return gets you there in about 25 years. (That's about the average 100-bagger in my study.)

But there are other ingredients as well. "Our analysis of the 100x stocks suggests that their essence lies in the alchemy of five elements forming the acronym SQGLP," they wrote:

- S—Size is small.
- Q—Quality is high for both business and management.
- G—Growth in earnings is high.
- L—Longevity in both Q and G
- P—Price is favorable for good returns.

Most of these are fairly objective, save for assessing management. "In the ultimate analysis, it is the management alone which is the 100x alchemist," they concluded. "And it is to those who have mastered the art of evaluating the alchemist that the stock market rewards with gold."

That's one reason why I focus on people, which we'll get into more in a later chapter. Investing with top entrepreneurs and owner-operators gives you a big edge. And when you mix that talent with the other elements, you are on your way to big returns, if not 100-baggerdom.

You can find the 48-page report on Indian 100-baggers free online. Just search for "Motilal Oswal 100x" and it will come right up.

Martelli's 10-Baggers

Another study forwarded to me by its author is a 45-slide presentation called "10x Return Stocks in the Last 15 Years," by Kevin Martelli at Martek Partners. Martelli presented it at the Value Investing Seminar in Trani, Italy, July 17–18, 2014.

Although not focused on 100-baggers, he found his inspiration in the same place I did: in Thomas Phelps's book *100 to 1 in the Stock Market*. Martelli cited George F. Baker's (1840–1931) dictum, mentioned in Phelps's book, that summarizes the idea:

To make money in stocks you must have "the vision to see them, the courage to buy them and the patience to hold them." According to Phelps, "patience is the rarest of the three."

Martelli's study, as the title suggests, looked at 10-baggers over the last 15 years. He screened from about 21,000 listed companies with a market cap of at least $100 million.

Out of this sample, he discovered 3,795 stocks (18 percent of the initial sample) that returned 10 times.

He found, as I have, that many were unpredictable. So he selected "with a great degree of subjectivity" a sample of "100 more predictable multibagger stocks, which a rational and long-term-oriented investor had a 'reasonable chance' to identify, purchase and hold over the long term."

It's a good study. Some conclusions:

- There is no magic formula to find long-term multibaggers.
- A low entry price relative to the company's long-term profit potential is critical.
- Small is beautiful: 68 percent of multibaggers in the selected sample were trading below a $300 million market cap at their low. (They were microcaps.)
- Great stocks often offer extensive periods during which to buy them.
- Patience is critical.

I'd add that many of his chosen stocks had top-management teams that made good capital decisions about how to invest company resources. There was often a large shareholder or an entrepreneurial founder involved. These can overcome the growth hurdle.

One interesting example here is AutoZone. It was a 24-bagger in Martelli's study despite registering ho-hum growth rates of 2–5 percent. Yet AutoZone bought back huge sums of stock, which powered earnings-per-share growth of 25 percent a year.

This is a topic we'll tackle more in chapter 11.

Heiserman's Earnings Staircase

Another study is by Hewitt Heiserman Jr., titled "Ben Graham and the Growth Investor." Heiserman forwarded me his 50-slide presentation. He started by recognizing the attractions of investing in a powerful grower and sitting on your investment. A few of these attractions are the following:

- You can defer capital gains.
- You can trade less.
- You don't have to worry about "timing."

Heiserman's study is not a 100-bagger study, but his emphasis is on growth stocks that became multibaggers.

But what about all those studies that show how value investing beats growth investing?

Well, that's because of the traps. An obvious trap is that investors often overpay for growth. It might seem with 100-baggers that you don't have to worry about the price you pay. But a simple mental experiment shows this isn't quite right.

Let's say we have two companies, A and B. Both start with $1 in earnings per share. Both will earn $20 in earnings per share in their twentieth year. And let's say at the end of year 10, both stocks will trade for $500 per share, or 25 times earnings.

Now, let's say in year one you can buy A for 5 times earnings, or $5 per share. And B you can buy for 50 times earnings, or $50. At the end of 20 years, you'll have a 100-bagger in A. Earnings will have gone up twentyfold and the price–earnings ratio fivefold. The combination gets you a 100-bagger.

In B, you'll have a 10-bagger after 20 years. That's not bad, but it's way worse than a 100-bagger. A $10,000 investment in A will turn into $1 million at the end of 20 years. A $10,000 investment in B will become $100,000.

So, it may seem that the price paid did not matter. Certainly, few would complain about a 10-bagger. But the truly big return comes when you have both earnings growth and a rising multiple. Ideally, you'd have both working for you.

My thought experiment might be extreme, but it serves to make the point that you can't just willy-nilly buy pricey growth stocks and expect to come up with 100-baggers.

Another trap is that earnings alone has many limitations. Heiserman shows the following:

1. Earnings omits investment in *fixed capital,* so when capital expenditures are greater than depreciation, the net cash drain is excluded.
2. Earnings omits investment in working capital, so when receivables and inventory grow faster than payables and accrued expenses, the net cash drain is excluded.
3. *Intangible growth-producing initiatives* such as R&D, promo/ advertising and employee education are expenses (i.e., not investments), even though the benefits will last for several accounting periods.
4. *Stockholders' equity* is free even though owners have an opportunity cost. (In other words, companies can spend $50 to create $1 in earnings. If all you look at is earnings per share, then you will ignore the cost to generate those earnings.)

The point here is you can't focus on earnings alone.

I don't want to get into the ins and outs of accounting and security analysis in this book. For one thing, there are plenty of basic books that will teach you why the above is true. Phelps recommended Benjamin Graham and David Dodd's *Security Analysis* for those who want a textbook on security analysis. And 43 years later, that recommendation is still a good one. But secondly, the quest for 100-baggers isn't about security analysis per se.

Conceptual power is more important. There is no amount of security analysis that is going to tell you a stock can be a 100-bagger. It takes vision and imagination and a forward-looking view into what a business can achieve and how big it can get. Investing is a reductionist art, and he who can boil things down to the essential wins.

What security analysis can do is weed out the duds—those companies that don't create value even though they show great growth in earnings. I'll have shortcuts to ways of thinking about these problems later in the book.

But to get back to Heiserman. Heiserman found a bunch of great examples of multibaggers. It reads like a "greatest hits" collection from the stock market: Microsoft, Cisco, Dell, Chico's, Google, Paychex, Hansen and more.

He says earnings just seem to step higher and higher, like going up a staircase.

All of these studies show us that past multibaggers enjoyed strong growth for a long time.

In the next chapter, let's look at what I discovered when I looked at that population of 100-baggers I pulled from 1962 through 2014.

CHAPTER 5:

THE 100-BAGGERS OF THE LAST 50 YEARS

At this point in our study, we've already accomplished a lot. I've introduced you to the remarkable Thomas Phelps and some of his wisdom and ideas. You've also seen how ordinary people can achieve the lofty returns of 100-baggerdom by simply holding onto good stocks. And we've traced out the basic outlines of what a 100-bagger looks like.

A 100-bagger is the product of time and growth. To net a 100-bagger, you need to hang onto a quality stock for a number of years. I like to emphasize the hard mathematical reality of turning $10,000 into $1 million. In fact, there is another fact about the pattern of 100-bagger returns you should know.

If you buy a stock that returns about 20 percent annually for 25 years, you'll get your 100-bagger. But if you sell in year 20, you'll get "only" about 40 to 1—before taxes. The last five years will more than double your overall return (assuming the annual return is constant). So, you must wait.

This is not to discourage you. You can earn great returns in less than 20 years. But I want to get you to think big.

As an aside, holding on is the most tax-efficient way to invest since you don't pay taxes on any gains—instead allowing gains to compound tax-free. Consider an example, courtesy of Chuck Akre, whom I mentioned in the first chapter.

Let's say Mr. Jones and Mr. Smith each invest $1 million in Berkshire Hathaway in 1977—a superpowered stock that gets its own chapter in this book, chapter 9. But let's say Jones likes to take his gains. So he sells the stock, only to buy it back the next day. Let's say Jones has a 33 percent combined tax liability at the federal and state levels. Smith, by contrast, lets the stock ride.

At the end of 18 years, let's say they both sell their shares for good and they both pay their taxes. Smith now has 3.4 times more than Jones. Taxes matter, and 100-bagger investing is tax-efficient.

So, back to these 100-baggers.

Remember, you need growth—and lots of it—a fact I will repeat again and again. Ideally, you need it in both the size of the business and in the multiple the market puts on the stock, as we've seen—the twin engines, as I call them.

This means you can't buy a utility stock or large mature company—such as McDonald's or Walmart or IBM—and expect anything close to a 100-bagger anytime soon (if ever). Finding what will become a 100-bagger is as much about knowing what not to buy as it is about knowing what to buy. The universe of what won't work is large. Knocking out huge chunks of that universe will help make your search for 100-baggers easier.

So, with that groundwork, we are now ready to look at the 100-baggers of the last 50 years—actually 52 years, but 50 has a nicer ring to it—and begin to answer the tough question "How can we find the next 100-baggers?"

Let's begin with some highlights on this 100-bagger population of 365 I've turned up using data from Compustat (which goes back as far as 1962).

The first thing I'd impress upon you is the tremendous diversity in the names. (You'll find the entire list and the companies' total returns in the appendix.) For example, here are the top 10 performers on the next page:

Company Name	Data Date	Total Return	Year to 100
Berkshire Hathaway	9/30/65	18,261	19.0
Kansas City Southern	12/31/72	16,931	18.2
Altria Group Inc	12/31/62	15,120	24.2
Wal-Mart Stores Inc	10/31/70	12,382	12.5
Hollyfrontier Corp	10/31/66	12,279	21.2
Franklin Resources Inc	12/31/81	11,363	4.2
Forest Laboratories—CL A	12/31/72	7,874	11.5
TJX Companies Inc	10/31/62	6,946	28.5
Southwest Airlines	12/31/71	5,478	9.5
Newmarket Corp	12/31/62	5,077	22.8

Berkshire is in a category by itself, and we'll look at it in more detail in chapter 9.

Kansas City Southern is a railroad stock. It's up more than 16,000-fold since 1974. A $10,000 investment there turned into $160 million in 40 years. I would never have guessed a railroad stock would top the list. The second stock on the list is an oil-and-gas firm that now is mainly a refiner. It's a 14,000-bagger.

Some of the other names are not so surprising. Walmart and McDonald's are stocks you probably could've guessed. And remember, this is just the top. There are 365 stocks that have met our 100-bagger threshold since 1962.

The 100-bagger population seems to favor no particular industry. There are retailers, beverage makers, food processors, tech firms and many other kinds. The only thing they seem to have in common is the subject of the study: they returned at least 100 to 1.

It's also worth considering the size of these companies when they started their march. Now I hesitate to make generalizations from the statistics, as I've said. And that's why my focus is more on anecdotal evidence and the ideas or theories behind 100-baggers. With that warning, I'll add that the median sales figure for the 365 names at the start was about $170 million and the median market cap was about $500 million.

That's interesting on two levels: One, it dispels a myth that to get a 100-bagger you have to start with tiny companies. True, these are small companies. But $170 million in sales is a substantial business in any era. It's not a tiny 50-cent stock with no revenues or barely any revenues.

Secondly, these figures imply a median price-to-sales ratio of nearly three, which isn't classically cheap by any measure. Going through these 100-baggers, you'll find stocks that looked cheap, but more often you find stocks that did not seem cheap *based on past results alone.*

So you must look forward to find 100-baggers. You have to train your mind to look for ideas that could be big, to think about the size of a company now versus what it could be. This doesn't mean you have to have a huge market to address, although that helps. Even a small company can become a 100-bagger by dominating a niche. Polaris was a 100-bagger and makes snowmobiles.

Despite occasional exceptions, you do want to focus on companies that have national or international markets. Far more common than niche companies on the 100-bagger list are companies such as Comcast, Aflac, Dollar General, ADP and Lockheed Martin. These companies came to dominate big spaces, though they all started small.

In 1982, Aflac had just $585 million in sales. By 2002, by which time it was a 100-bagger, Aflac had sales of $10.2 billion. Aflac's price-to-sales ratio, by the way, went from about 1.7 to 5.4. So, you had the twin engines: sales growth and multiple growth. Sales went up roughly 17-fold and the price-to-sales ratio went up roughly 3-fold. In combination, and including reinvested dividends, they worked the stock up a hundredfold. Even if we exclude the dividends, Aflac became a 100-bagger two years later, in 2004.

Another interesting chart to look at concerns how long these stocks took to become 100-baggers. The average time was 26 years. That was also the median. I divided the time-to-100-bagger stats up in 15-year increments and you can see the results.

Total 100-baggers by year-range

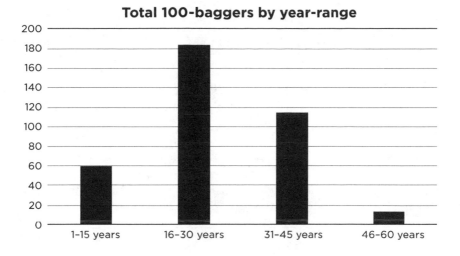

The fastest to 100-baggerdom

Company Name	Years to 100
Franklin Resources Inc	4.2
Pharmacyclics Inc	5.0
Nexstar Broadcasting Group	5.0
Questcor Pharmaceuticals Inc	5.0
Biogen Idec Inc	5.5
Time Warner Inc	6.0
Valeant Pharmaceuticals Intl	6.5
Dell Inc	7.2
L Brands Inc	7.3
Qualcomm Inc	7.3
Cisco Systems Inc	7.3
Emc Corp/MA	7.7
Henry (Jack) & Associate	8.3
Vector Group Ltd	8.5
Edwards (A G) Inc	8.7
Hasbro Inc	9.5
Monster Beverage Corp	9.5
Southwest Airlines	9.5
Home Depot Inc	9.7
NVR Inc	9.7

Case Studies

Let's look at some case studies of 100-baggers. This is a way to capture, most vividly, what it took to get to 100x.

For these case studies, I had some help from analysts at Agora Financial: Alejandro Lopez de Haro, Matthew Goodman (a.k.a. "Yoda") and Thompson Clark. You'll meet them below.

Monster Beverage

We'll start with a deep look at Monster Beverage, the famous maker of energy drinks and other beverages. Monster became a 100-bagger in under 10 years. It hit the mark in 2006 and kept on going, turning into a 700+-bagger by the end of 2014.

Yoda, one of the three analysts I mentioned above, prepared a case study on Monster. The story starts with a pair of immigrant entrepreneurs. Hilton Schlosberg and Rodney Sacks came to California from South Africa. Both would become billionaires.

Hilton and Rodney paid $14.5 million for Hansen's Natural Soda and Apple Juice in 1992, Yoda reports. Hansen's had a long history going back to the 1930s. What started as a business to sell fresh unpasteurized juices was ironically later turned into a business that sold shelf-stabilized pasteurized juices by the founder's grandson.

Hansen's had no best-selling product. It barely even had distribution in much of the country. But Hilton and Rodney wanted it to become a marketing and branding corporation, with no in-house manufacturing—like Coca-Cola. As early as their 2001 proxy, they made clear that "the company is concentrating on marketing carbonated functional drinks, in particular, energy drinks."

"Their initial launch of Hansen Energy quickly became popular but flamed out as Red Bull became the force we know today," Yoda writes. "It left Hansen in the dust but provided some lessons that would later propel some of their finest decisions."

For one thing, they decided to slim down their offerings. In 1999 and 2000, the list of products they had was almost absurd, as Yoda relates:

Signature Sodas in 14-ounce glass bottles, Slim Down in 8.2oz cans, 13.5-oz glass bottle smoothies, 64 oz P. E.T. plastic bottled smoothies, 11.5-ounce cans of premium functional smoothies, licensing brands and trademarks, 100% juice in glass bottles, childrens multi-vitamin drinks in 8.45-oz aseptic packaging, "gold standard" green tea in proprietary 20-oz bottles, food bars, GMO-free cereal, etc., etc., etc., (etc.!!!)!

In 2002, they introduced Monster Energy, which became a focus. And in a 2003 conference call, they said, "We have pulled back a little bit this year on new products."

"They were very crafty in how they approached it," Yoda writes, "with their 2002 annual report revealing that 'In connection with the development of new products and flavors, independent suppliers bear a large portion of the expense of product development, thereby enabling us to develop new products and flavors at relatively low cost.'"

Without any internal manufacturing, it was easy for them to test out different products in different packaging because they weren't bogged down with finding the time and money required to run a factory. "They felt strongly that differentiated brands were winning brands," Yoda writes. "As it would later turn out, packaging was a big part of their success."

As mentioned earlier, Hansen's got out to a great start with Hansen Energy, its 8-oz. offering, before losing out to Red Bull. Yoda dug up a response to a question on their Q4 2003 earnings call. The question was whether investors should expect a repeat of the success of Monster. Management said,

Firstly, I think we've learned a lot in the last seven years . . . When we started in energy, we came out and we competed initially with Red Bull. At that time, the size of the company was such that we probably didn't have enough manpower and marketing to put behind the brand . . . In hindsight, we probably should have put more behind it . . . [Red Bull] spent, for many years, disproportionately in the market to their sales, in order to establish the brand, *and they did a good job.* (emphasis Yoda's)

In introducing Monster, Hansen's did not repeat its mistake. Just look at the number of sales and marketing people they added beginning in 2002 (when Monster was introduced):

	2001	2002	2003	2004	2005	2006
Sales & marketing employees	66	63	114	217	363	591

"They spent heavily on promotions, marketing campaigns, and sales & marketing employees," Yoda writes. "Monster and Rockstar entered the category at about the same time in the 16oz niche. Being one of the two pioneers, Monster recognized and seized on the opportunity."

Of course, Hansen's didn't "just" spend its time and money on branding and marketing and new-product introductions. They also spent a lot of time focusing on product distribution and the different ways to both reach consumers and earn valuable shelf space with retailers.

"In its early years, in many ways it would be appropriate to call them a think tank," Yoda writes. "They tried different ways to reach consumers. For their Juice Slam product, they partnered with Costco. With their E2O Energy Water, they tried to sell directly to retail customers. They even put in the lowest bid on a WIC program (similar to food stamps) that gave them the exclusive right to make 100% of the allotted apple juice and mixed fruit juice that the program offers in WIC-approved grocers."

The WIC contract got them in grocery stores that hadn't stocked the company's products before. It opened doors, in other words, for Hansen's products and for ways to create brand awareness.

When they decided to roll out a new energy-drink line, Lost Energy, they again experimented. Instead of going through their regular distribution channel, they decided to use the Dr. Pepper / 7-Up network.

They also took advantage of their brand identity. "Their studies showed that drinkers of 16oz energy beverages tended to be men," Yoda writes. No surprise, given their black can and bear-clawed M. "They also found that using words like 'sugar free,' or 'diet' were perceived to be feminine, along with light/white/silver colored cans; according to their data.

So when introduced their diet Monster beverage, they kept the can black, changed the *M* to blue, and name it Lo-Carb. It was an instant success."

Another genius aspect of Monster Lo-Carb was that it was a much easier sale, as Monster itself was already very popular. They figured out that the only way to get shelf space for a second product is to make sure your first product is in very high demand. "And without shelf space for your products you are just a couple of people with ideas," Yoda writes, "and a warehouse full of beverages. Monster Lo-Carb was one of the first rollouts that really needed almost no promotional support."

This was all part of the effort to create a brand, which is particularly important in beverages. This all started to pay off in rapid sales growth:

	2002	2003	2004	2005	2006
Sales & marketing employees	112,885	135,655	224,098	415,417	696,322
Net sales	92,046	110,352	180,341	348,886	605,774
NS % of gross	81.54%	81.35%	80.47%	83.98%	87.00%
Gross profit % of NS	34.80%	39.70%	46.30%	52.30%	52.30%

"But there is an even more exciting part," Yoda writes. "If you have a brand that catches on, grows, and hits scale, the costs start to slowly unwind."

Note two things from the above:

1. Net sales grew to a larger percentage of gross sales. That re-flects promotions (discounts) Monster no longer needed to offer, as Monster was now a well-known brand retailers wanted to carry.

2. Gross profits as a percentage of net sales also increased as their copackers and distribution partners started to see them as a good customer and offer concessions to stay.

"This is a pretty potent cocktail, and led to the dramatic rise in share price," Yoda writes. "Look at the effect that this extra margin has on the bottom line."

	2002	2003	2004	2005	2006
Operating Income	5,293	9,826	33,886	103,443	158,579
Net Income	3,029	5,930	20,387	62,775	97,949
EPS	0.04	0.07	0.22	0.65	0.99
Long-term debt	3,837	602	583	525	303
Shareholder equity	28,371	35,050	58,571	125,509	225,084
ROE	10.68%	16.92%	34.81%	50.02%	43.52%

Note: ROE is Return on Equity. Its net income divided by shareholder equity

For all the detailed financial analysis in this case study, the essence of the deal is right here in this table. You see a rapid increase in sales, rising profits and a rising ROE. (We'll get to ROE in chapter 6.) If there is a detectable formula for 100-baggerdom, this is it.

You could've bought shares in 2004, well along in the story, and still made 100 times your money. You didn't have to do all the deep financial work on display here. In fact, it probably would have helped if you didn't because a lot of smart financial people said it wouldn't work. But more on that in a bit.

"It is easy to see the business quality when studying the above table," Yoda writes. "So why didn't everyone get rich? Very few people followed the story early on."

	Q2'03	Q3'03	Q4'04	Q1'04	Q2'04
# of analysts of conference calls	1	1	3	4	8

And even if you knew the story, you had to hold on—even if you looked silly and even if sophisticated people told you it wouldn't work.

The Value Investors Club is a widely followed stock-research platform full of sophisticated people. And in 2005, an author using a pen name posted Hansen's as a short—that is, betting against it. This poster had won the VIC competition three times—which, Yoda believes, must be "one of the best records ever."

So, he was not some unknown in damning Hansen's.

"The write-up was well received by this distinguished group of investors," Yoda writes. "One even chimed in: 'No strategic player is going to buy this company. It is a clearly overvalued, marginal player in a fad business that has a very average brand with no distribution edge. . . .' The author wrote this up at a split-adjusted price of $6.31. Not only did Hansen never trade as low as $6.31 again, but inside of 12 months the stock was at $26!"

The company changed its name to Monster Beverage, its now signature product, in 2012.

Looking at historical results, it's interesting to note that Monster never really got expensive, despite its reputation as a "high flyer." Its price–earnings ratio was never out of line with its growth rate.

Year	2005	2006	2007	2008	2009	2010	2011	2012	2013	2014
P/E	28x	30x	29x	30x	17x	23x	30x	28x	35x	39x
% EPS growth	218%	60%	36%	-27%	99%	3%	34%	22%	5%	42%

Monster shows us the power of high sales growth and building a brand and the potent mix of high sales growth and rising profit margins and rising return on equity. It also shows you how independent-minded you had to be. There was no shortage of smart people telling you why Monster wouldn't work.

But it did work—and in spectacular fashion.

Amazon

Next up is a name that will not need much of an introduction: Amazon.

The online retailing giant was a 100-bagger more than twice over. Thompson Clark, one of the analysts I mentioned earlier, prepared the case study on Amazon, and what he found will surprise you. He's cracked the code of what makes Amazon great.

Amazon was one you could've bought right out of the gate. Shares started trading in May of 1997. After adjusting for stock splits, your effective purchase price was $1.50. "Before the century was done, you had your 100 bagger," Thompson writes. "Shares hit a high of $221 in April of 1999. Your gains were a cool, 14,633%. A 146-bagger."

But that return was so fleeting, it doesn't "count" for purposes of our study—which uses year-end data. Amazon wouldn't see a price that high for more than a decade. "Amazon was, as you might imagine, not spared by the dot-com bust," Thompson points out. "Shares fell back to earth, touching single digits by the middle of 2001."

Looked at through the lens of our study, Amazon took about 13 years to turn into a 100-bagger. And by May of 2015, you were sitting on gains of 28,300 percent, or a 283-bagger.

So, how did Amazon do it?

Let's start with Jeff Bezos because this is a case where you had one of the great owner-operators at the helm. Bezos is currently 51 years old and owns 18 percent of the company, of which he is both CEO and chairman of the board.

"There are no signs he's leaving, either," Thompson writes. "In a 2014 Business Insider interview, Bezos, perhaps channeling Mr. Buffett, said 'I still run into work.'" He loves what he does.

He started the company when he was 30. He used to work at DE Shaw, an investment-management company. Importantly, he's not a programmer like Bill Gates. As Thompson says, "He's a Wall Street guy in a lot of ways."

"At heart, he understands two things," Thompson writes. "He understands the value of a business is the sum of its future free cash flows, discounted back to the present. And he understands capital allocation and the importance of return on invested capital."

The latter, as we've seen—and will see more of later—is critical to 100-baggerdom. Thompson marshals some good evidence on Bezos's thinking, highlighting the key phrases:

- From Bezos's 1999 shareholder letter: "Each of the previous goals I've outlined contribute to our long-standing objective of building the best, most profitable, *highest return on capital*, long-term franchise."
- From Bezos's first shareholder letter, in 1997: "Market leadership can translate directly to higher revenue, higher profitability,

greater capital velocity and correspondingly stronger *returns on invested capital*. Our decisions have *consistently reflected this focus."*

He has a relentless focus on the long term. "Every year," Thompson adds, "he includes his 1997 shareholder letter at the end of the current year letter. The point he's trying to emphasize: it's all about the long term."

So, we all know Amazon came to dominate online retailing. The question is, could you have come up with a sound argument to buy Amazon based on fundamentals *before* it became a 100-bagger?

Thompson argues for an emphatic yes. And I agree with his reasoning.

Before I get to that, I want to start with a big-picture observation. Thompson shared a chart that I found truly remarkable and thought about for several minutes as the implications rushed through my head. See the chart below, which reveals the growth of e-commerce as a percentage of overall US retail sales.

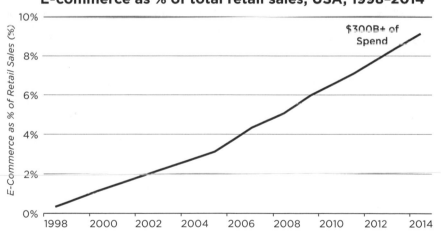

E-commerce as % of total retail sales, USA, 1998–2014

It almost seems obvious now, but was it so hard to imagine back in 1998 or 2002 that Internet sales would someday make up more than sub-2 percent of retail sales? Seeing this makes me wonder where my head was. (I never owned Amazon, despite being a heavy user of its services.)

And what's incredible about it is that even today, only *9 percent* of all US retail sales happen over the Internet. Amazon started when this was almost nothing. Even now, is it a stretch to think Internet sales could make up 35 percent of all retail sales or even half? Maybe this 100-bagger has a long way to go.

But to get back to Thompson's analysis. . . .

"First, there's an important myth to dispel about Amazon," Thompson writes. "The consensus opinion is pretty clear: Amazon does not make money. Is that true? Absolutely not."

Remember Bezos's first shareholder letter in 1997. He emphasized return on invested capital and investing for the future. One way Amazon does this is by spending a lot on research and development—which is a form of investment.

"I went through Amazon's historical results," Thompson wrote. "Which, by the way, are fantastic. Sales have grown at a compounded annual rate of over 40% since the [sic] 1997."

So here, again, we see those important ingredients: growth, growth and more growth!

"Looking at Amazon's reported operating income, it doesn't look profitable," Thompson continues. "On $88 billion in 2014 sales, Amazon earned a measly $178 million in operating income. That's a razor-thin 0.20% operating margin.

"Adding back R&D, however, paints a completely different picture. In 2014, Amazon spent $9.2 billion on R&D. Adding that back to operating income, Amazon generated adjusted operating income of $9.4 billion in 2014. That's an operating margin of 10.6%.

"Very impressive. And what's even more impressive is how consistent this trend is."

Thompson created the table on the next page.

Adding back R&D may sound crazy, but the point is to think of R&D as an investment in this case. (There is a long history of debate in accounting circles about how to treat R&D. Should it be expensed against sales? Or should it be capitalized on the balance sheet like property and depreciated—or amortized—over time in bits?)

	1996	1997	1998	1999	2000	2001	2002
Sales	$15.75	$148	$609	$1,639	$2,761	$3,122	$3,933
Growth (%)		838.06%	312.30%	189.13%	68.45%	13.07%	25.98%
Operating Income	-6	-32	-109	-605	-863	-412	64
Operating Income (%)	-38.10%	-21.66%	-17.90%	-36.91%	-31.26%	-13.20%	1.63%
Plus: R&D	2	13	46	159	269	241	215
Adj. EBIT	-4	-19	-63	-446	-594	-171	279
Adj. Operating Income (%)	-25.40%	-12.86%	-10.34%	-27.21%	-21.51%	-5.46%	-7.09%

	2003	2004	2005	2006	2007	2008	2009
Sales	$5,264	$6,921	$8,490	$10,711	$14,835	$19,166	$24,509
Growth (%)	33.84%	31.48%	22.87%	26.18%	38.50%	29.19%	27.88%
Operating Income	270	440	432	389	655	842	1129
Operating Income (%)	5.13%	6.36%	5.09%	3.63%	4.42%	4.39%	4.61%
Plus: R&D	257	263	451	662	818	1033	1240
Adj. EBIT	527	723	883	10.51	1473	1875	2369
Adj. Operating Income (%)	10.01%	10.45%	10.40%	9.81%	9.93%	9.78%	9.67%

	2010	2011	2012	2013	2014
Sales	$34,384	$48,077	$61,093	$74,452	$88,968
Growth (%)	40.29%	39.82%	27.07%	21.87%	19.52%
Operating Income	1406	862	676	745	178
Operating Income (%)	4.09%	1.79%	1.11%	1.00%	0.20%
Plus: R&D	1734	2909	4564	6585	9275
Adj FBIT	3140	3771	5240	7310	9453
Adj. Operating Income (%)	9.13%	7.81%	8.58%	9.82%	10.62%

"My higher level point is simply that Amazon could have been profitable if it wanted to," Thompson writes. "If it wanted to show earnings, it could have. It didn't. The layman who might be interested in buying Amazon stock would certainly be turned off by its lack of ever being profitable. Well, if you back out R&D—effectively backing out capex—you see how profitable it really has been."

He recognizes to do this properly you'd want to amortize those R&D costs over some time period, the same way a firm would amortize costs spent on equipment. There is some component of R&D that is essential to keep Amazon going, but there is also a growth component that helps generate future sales. "What's the mix between growth and maintenance R&D?" Thompson asks. "No idea, but it's an important question and worth discussing."

For purposes of this exercise, let's just look at R&D as an investment Amazon makes to grow its business. Since 2003, as Thompson notes, operating margin excluding R&D has been almost exactly 10 percent. "Now, could a savvy fundamental investor ever have made the case for Amazon?" Thompson asked. "Sure."

Let's go back to early 2003:

- $21.94 share price
- enterprise value = $8.3 billion
- 2002 sales of $3.9 billion
- 2002 earnings before interest and taxes, ex-R&D = $279 million
- 2002 adjusted operating margin = 7 percent
- EV/EBIT = 33, an extremely steep multiple

"At this point though," Thompson adds, "a tiny fraction of the United States was online. And an even-tinier fraction of retail sales was made online. In other words, the runway was massive." (See that chart on page 55.)

"Let's say you projected sales growth of 30% per year," Thompson continues. "Your 2005 Sales target would be = $7.6B. Put a 10% margin on that, consistent with the trend of EBIT ex-R&D. You'd be buying Amazon right at 10 times 2005 operating income ex-R&D. That's a very conservative multiple."

I pause here to note this wouldn't have been easy, but it would have been possible to think about.

"Along with earnings growth, share price had grown as well," Thompson says. "Your $21.94 investment had risen to $43.92 by February of 2006. That's a double in three years, for a compounded annual growth rate of 26%. And over that same period you would have crushed the S&P 500, which had risen half that at just 50%, or 14.3% per year.

"By 2006 you were along for the *long* ride. Hanging on to shares up until May of 2015 would have netted you a 15-bagger, or a compounded 26% annualized return. Once again, extremely impressive."

So it would not have been easy to net a 100-bagger on Amazon. You would have to have had a strong conviction early that as an idea it would work. And you would have had to sit through a soul-crushing decline, where it lost more than 80 percent of its value.

But you also would have had many chances to buy it at those low prices such that, while you might not have netted a 100-bagger, you could easily have been up fiftyfold. And Amazon is not done.

You had to have trusted Bezos, and you had to have been clued into his thinking. If he wanted to, Bezos could cut R&D expenses, and Amazon would gush cash. Instead, he invests the money and creates new growth.

Thompson sums it up this way:

> If you trust in Bezos, you're okay with the company having razor thin operating margins. In 2014, operating margins were 0.20%. Adding back R&D, however, gets you an adjusted operating margin of 10%. I showed in the table above how remarkably consistent this trend is.

> Making a fundamental case for Amazon, and getting a 100-bagger, would be very hard to do. Your best bet was to buy at the IPO and bet purely on growing retail sales. That chart on internet sales and trust in Bezos would be the keys to your thesis.

> I make the fundamental case that in February of 2003, you could have bought Amazon based on trailing numbers and conservative assumptions. That would have brought your gains to 15x, or 26% compounded in 2014.

Thompson goes further and thinks that Amazon may be a buy even today. I'll share his analysis in the nearby table. Based on today's price, his analysis gets you a 127 percent return, or a compound annual return of 31 percent over the next 3 years.

"The biggest point to convey," Thompson wraps up, "is that return on capital is extremely important. If a company can continue to reinvest at high rates of return, the stock (and earnings) compound . . . getting you that parabolic effect."

It's a point we will return to again and again.

Price on 5/28/25	$427
Enterprise Value	$196,807
2014 Results	
Sales	$88,988
Adj. Operating Income	$9453
Adj. Operating Margin	*11%*
Assumptions:	
Sales Grow at 20% per year	
Adj. Operating Margins hit 15%	
Sales	$153,771
Operating Margin	15%
EBIT	$230,656
2017 EV/EBIT	**8.5%**
2017 Valuation	
Adj. EBIT	$23,066
Multiple	20
Fair Value	$461,313
Shares Out	476
Fair Value per Share	$969
Price Today	$427
Upside	**127%**
# Periods	3
CAGR	*31%*

At this point, I have a few more case studies to share with fewer financial details but that nonetheless serve to illustrate the essential characteristic of 100-baggers: you need to have a long runway to grow. Alejandro, one of the analysts I mentioned earlier, prepared the following case studies.

Electronic Arts

An American entrepreneur named Trip Hawkins started Electronic Arts (EA) after leaving his post as a director of strategy and marketing at Apple Computer in 1982. Based in Redwood City, CA, the company develops and publishes video games.

EA became a 100-bagger in just 14 years. It hit the mark in 2004—and kept going. Here Alejandro did the research on EA.

"The video game industry is still relatively young (40 years or so) and remains incredibly competitive," Alejandro writes. "Founding members of this multibillion dollar industry have faltered and been overtaken by new players."

He points out that the founding titans such as Atari and Sega no longer dominate as they once did. Even Nintendo has lost some of its competitive edge to newer players.

"Sony (PlayStation) and Microsoft (Xbox) have become the dominant players for the console market," Alejandro writes. "But they face increasing competition from game developers who skip the console route. The latter instead go directly to consumers via the internet or through apps.

"Therefore," Alejandro continues, "it's extremely interesting to dissect Electronic Arts, an American video game developer, and its path to 100-bagger status. Its success provides insights into how to succeed when faced with the uncertainty of both technology and fickle human tastes."

It seemed to do this by creating hit after hit, and by securing key licenses to valuable franchises, thereby keeping competitors out.

First, you can see the unpredictable nature of the business in its erratic profitability. Profit margins and return on assets jumped around quite a bit from year to year, following game hits and misses and new or update releases.

EA's wild profit ride

Date	Profit margins	ROA
12/31/90	8.5%	13.2%
12/31/91	10%	17.5%
12/31/92	10.6%	17.3%
12/31/93	10.6%	17.2%
12/31/94	11%	156%
12/31/95	8.7%	10.7%
12/31/96	76%	8.5%
12/31/97	7.9%	8.7%
12/31/98	5.8%	7%
12/31/99	9.6%	11.5%
12/31/00	0.8%	0.8%
12/31/01	2.3%	2.1%
12/31/02	14.2%	14.4%
12/31/03	17.6%	14.9%
12/31/04	18.5%	13.2%
12/31/05	9%	6%
12/31/06	2.7%	1.7%

"Unlike many of today's tech companies," Alejandro writes, "EA focused on its bottom line. One of the early examples of EA's ability to protect margins was to avoid existing distribution partners. Instead they opted to deal directly with retailers, which gave them better margins."

EA experimented with different forms of packaging. For example, EA used album style packaging for games in the early 1980s such as *M.U.L.E.* and *Pinball Construction Set*. "This type of packaging was pioneered by EA because the record album style could save costs," as Alejandro points out.

EA also focused on making games for all consoles, so it skipped out on the costly and competitive console-hardware segment. EA's executives still credit this strategy as a foundation of their business success today.

Whatever you choose to emphasize, EA pushed the right buttons. In 1990, sales were just $96 million. By 2004, sales were $3.1 billion. That's a 32-fold increase. The multiple the market put on those sales also exploded—from 2.7 in 1990 to 13 by 2004.

Earnings also popped. Earnings totaled $8 million in 1990. By 2004, they were $586 million. That's a 73-fold increase. And the price–earnings ratio went from about 12 to 32.

For those kinds of numbers, EA needed more than smart packaging and games for all consoles. It needed to create games people wanted.

"EA's founders chose this name, so the story goes, because they wanted to promote their games as a kind of art," Alejandro writes. "Art in an almost Hollywood type sense as some believe the name was actually inspired by the legendary United Artists studio."

EA treated its game developers like rock stars. EA gave its developers personal credit for the creation of a game. This "was allegedly done through not just financial incentives but also PR type activities that celebrated them along with their work," Alejandro says. He continues: "The album covers for the games in 1980's also reinforce the idea that these games and their creators were something more than geeks who had the capacity to make playful images on a screen. All of this focus on quality lead to some very successful games."

This is especially true in sports, where EA's franchise is basically un-rivaled. I grew up in the 1980s, and I can still recall their tagline "EA Sports. If it's in the game, it's in the game!" and how we spent hours playing *Madden Football* in college.

"The realism of their games has basically outflanked most other sports games out there," Alejandro writes. "This has in turn led them to have exclusive rights to the development of games for several professional leagues along with that of their players. Madden NFL, NBA Live, FIFA, NHL and PGA Tour series have all been produced under the EA sports label since the late 80s and early 90's. FIFA, its most successful sports franchise, broke its 100 million unit sale in 2010."

EA had other hit franchises too: *SimCity, Battlefield* and the *Need for Speed* series. "To have so many hit franchises under one roof is exactly why this company has consistently grown since its inception," Alejandro concludes.

EA is intriguing on many levels. It was in what seems a fickle industry but managed to create a culture that produced winning games. And you see here what you'll see with nearly all of the 100-baggers—explosive growth in sales. Added to this, EA had healthy, if erratic, earnings and profit margins.

This is one where you had to believe in the story and think big. Which is also required for 100-baggerdom.

Comcast

Ralph Roberts transformed what was a tiny Mississippi cable company into the industry giant we know today as Comcast. The roots of the story go back to the 1960s. According the *Wall Street Journal* obituary of Roberts (who died in June of 2015):

> Cable television, in those days, was still a tiny business of community antennas and strung-up wires. Mr. Roberts got wind of it through a chance meeting with a cable-system owner who was looking to get a struggling Southern cable distributor off his hands. Smelling opportunity, Mr. Roberts made his first acquisition in 1963: a Tupelo, Miss., cable operator transmitting signals for 1,200 local residents.

The shares listed on the NASDAQ in 1972 and are up more than 100,000 percent since. This is one rare case where we have a great founder/operator, in Ralph Roberts. And then we have a second capable operator in his fourth son Brian Robert, who became president in 1990 and CEO in 2002.

For purposes of our study, we began the clock with the lows in 1981. From that point, it took almost 18 years to get to 100x.

Comcast is an interesting case study because, as with Amazon, you did not see steadily growing earnings. In fact, Comcast often reported losses as it spent heavily on building its cable systems.

You had to see beyond reported figures to understand the value of its subscriber network. Sticky customers who pay every month, year after year, formed the backbone of any Comcast investment thesis.

While you did not see earnings, what you did see was sales growth and growth in subscribers.

"In the 1980's and 1990's Comcast went through substantial growth because of various acquisitions," Alejandro writes. "For example, the purchase of a 26% stake of Group W Cable in 1986 doubled Comcast's number of subscribers to 1 million. While their acquisition of Maclean-Hunter's American division in 1994 allowed Comcast to reach a total of 3.5 million subscribers and made Comcast the third-largest operator in the United States."

It would keep going. In 1995, Comcast acquired E. W. Scripps Co. for $1.575 billion. The latter was a company with cable subscribers, and this pushed Comcast's total number of subscribers to 4.3 million.

"Comcast also began to diversify its portfolio of businesses," Alejandro writes. It acquired a majority stake of QVC, a home-shopping television network, for $2.1 billion in 1995.

Comcast would also become a player in the mobile and Internet industries. "First with their purchase of American Cellular Network Corporation, a regional mobile service, for $230 million in 1988," Alejandro writes. "The second took place in 1996 with their launch of the @HomeNetwork which offered internet services."

These efforts earned Comcast a $1 billion investment from Microsoft in 1997. "Comcast's integrated approach to cable distribution, programming and telecommunications complements that vision of linking PCs and TVs.

Today's announcement will enhance the integration of broadband pipes and content to expand the services offered to consumers," said Microsoft founder Bill Gates in a press release then.

The acquisitions continued. Two big ones were the 2001 acquisition of AT&T's cable system and in 2011 the acquisition of NBCUniversal.

Comcast's network also became an important highway for the Internet, and that propelled growth even further. You can see how Comcast's sales really began to build as we got into the late 1990s and early 2000s.

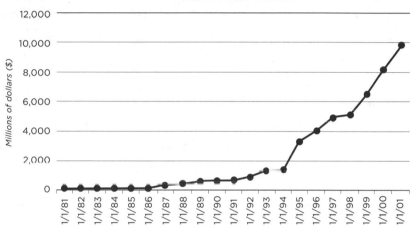

Sales at Comcast

What's most interesting is this was still early in the story. Comcast would eventually grow sales more than six times from 2001, as it continued to expand and acquire companies.

"Big acquisitions during this time include: AT&T Broadband, Adelphia (50–50 with TIME Warner Cable) and a 51 percent stake of NBCUniversal," Alejandro writes.

An investor would have had to sit through a nasty fall as the 2000 stock market bubble burst. Comcast shares would give up about half their value from the peak to the trough in 2002. But then it was off to the races once again.

An investor who held on through 2014 would've had a 188-bagger. This is a short case study, but it serves to highlight again the power of sales growth and the ability to see something beyond the reported earnings.

Netting a 100-bagger takes vision and tenacity and, often, a conviction in an idea that may not yet be obvious in the financials.

Pepsi

Pepsi is perhaps more typical of a 100-bagger you may uncover. It's a simple business with good margins that just grew and grew into big markets.

Pepsi is another case of a stock making the 100-bagger list in both Phelps's study and my own. In Phelps's book, the story begins with Loft Inc., which absorbed PepsiCo and rebranded itself as such in 1941. (There's a lot of interesting backstory here that would take us too far afield. But here's a bit of interesting trivia. Pepsi filed for bankruptcy twice: in 1923 and again in 1931.) According to Phelps, if you had bought the stock in 1938, your cost basis would have been 75 cents per share. That stake was worth $427 in 1971—a 569-bagger over 33 years.

In our study, the story picks up in 1962. "It took the New York-based soft drinks and snacks giant 28.5 years to hit 100-bagger status from 1962," Alejandro writes. "In fact, from 1962 to the late 1980s, the stock showed no signs of being a 100-bagger in the making."

But then it kicked off a huge international expansion. By 1985, Pepsi had a presence in close to 150 countries. "These include China," Alejandro writes, "which opened its doors to them that same year, as well as the Soviet Union, a decade earlier. These two nascent markets that would make Pepsico a lot of money over the next couple of decades."

Along the way, the company continued to introduce new products and expand its snack business. "In 1982," Alejandro writes, "Pepsi developed their Slice-brand, which made sodas with a small amount of fruit juice. This created a new market and thereby increasing its market share of the drinks industry."

In 1986, it got into fast-food, picking up KFC and Taco Bell. In 1989, PepsiCo acquired Britain-based Walkers Crisps and Smith Crisps, leading snack-food companies in the UK.

This list of international hits kept coming, per Alejandro:

- In 1990, PepsiCo signed its largest commercial trade agreement in history with the Soviet Union. The same year, PepsiCo gained a controlling interest in Gamesa, the largest cookie company in Mexico.

- In 1994, PepsiCo also expanded into Vietnam. This made it the first major soft drink maker to begin production and distribution within that country. It also formed a partnership with Starbucks to offer ready-made coffee drinks in the United States.
- In 1998, Pepsi entered into a joint agreement with Empresas Polar SA of Venezuela and became the biggest snack-chip dealer in Latin America. This deal was part of its 1995 plan to introduce its Lay products to an additional 20 markets around the world.

The list of acquisitions of new properties continued too: Aquafina in 1997, Tropicana in 1998.

Financially, I'm drawn to two facts. The first is Pepsi's consistently high gross profit margins of 57 percent or better. As we'll see later, in chapter 12, this is a clue to the competitive position of Pepsi.

And second, the sales and profit growth was remarkable over time—as we've come to expect. Sales in 1962 were just $192 million. By 2014, they were over $64 billion. And this doesn't include the eventual spin-out of YUM Brands. Likewise, net profits went from $15 million to over $6 billion.

Over the period covered by the study, PepsiCo returned more than 1,000-fold.

Gillette

Gillette took nearly 32 years to become a 100-bagger.

You know the company as the maker of razor blades. "Gillette," Alejandro writes, "which has been owned by Proctor and Gamble for the past 10 years, has been estimated to possess as much as 70 percent of the razor blade market."

Founded in 1901, the firm had a lot of success early. As an interesting side point, Phelps included Gillette in his book. The stock was a 100-bagger from 1943 to 1971. The cost in 1943 was just $4.75 and that would have grown to $364 per share by 1971. "Fortune's July 1962 issue named it the third most profitable company in America," Alejandro writes.

"In my research of 100-baggers," Alejandro continues, "I have seen that a constant desire to grow a business is a key characteristic." He found this trait throughout Gillette's history. It was always expanding into new markets and creating new products. Alejandro found Gillette's use of technology was important:

> One of the ways that they were able to do this so effectively was through their wise use of technology for the development and marketing of products. Throughout its history Gillette executives showed an understanding of technology that gave them an edge over their competitors. As Darwin said, "It is not the strongest or the most intelligent who will survive but those who can best manage change."

For example, Gillette was an early adopter in the use of television advertising.

"In 1944, when television was largely ignored by brands, Gillette executives took a gamble on it," Alejandro writes. And this greatly enhanced the visibility of Gillette's brand. Gillette didn't just spend money on advertising, either, but tracked sales using data. Ultimately, Gillette found it helped boost sales in those early years.

"Another technology play that benefitted Gillette was their decision to continuously work on improvements for their blades," Alejandro said. "They even did this when there is no sign of a competitor with a product that could take away a portion of their market."

This was partly because they found loyal customers who would pay more for a blade that was slightly better than the one they currently used. Alejandro cites a line from Peter K. Hoffman, president of Gillette's grooming division, in 2001: "History has shown there is a portion of the market that is anxious for our next innovation." This was something Gillette figured out early.

The focus on research and development also proved a tough moat for competitors to cross—even when it wasn't first to the market. Gillette could use its own patent portfolio to cut out competitors' blades.

"For example," Alejandro writes,

in 1962 Tiny Wilkinson Sword, Ltd., of London introduced a set of coated stainless steel blades with a lot of success. Users claimed that they could get at least a dozen smooth shaves from this product while they got only 3 or 4 from Gillette's carbon steel blades.

Wilkinson's blade could have seriously impacted Gillette's dominant position. However, Gillette researchers had actually patented the stainless steel coating process before Wilkinson could obtain a patent. So Gillette received a royalty for each stainless blade sold by Wilkinson. This crippled Wilkinson.

A year after the 'Wilkinson Shock' Gillette introduced it's own stainless steel blade in 1963. They priced it below Wilkinson and their American competitors. By doing this they would again essentially dominate the market and would launch yet another set of slightly improved blades a couple of years later.

Gillette was and is a great business. And yet. . . .

Looking at the first couple of decades of Gillette as a public company, you'd be hard-pressed to find signs that it would one day be a 100-bagger. In fact, for the first 20 years, the stock didn't advance all that much. It went up about 40 percent. That's it.

If you took all your dividends and reinvested them, you'd have had about $340 for every $100 you invested. That's much better, but not so hot for two decades. That's about 6.5 percent annualized—slow. Recall that even at a 10 percent annual return you'd need 48 years to turn a 100-bagger. Gillette's pace was only two-thirds of that.

"This is despite its consistent net income growth during this period," Alejandro points out. "The latter grew 3.5-fold." Part of the reason is valuation. Gillette did not get the benefits of the "twin engines." Earnings grew, but the multiple on those earnings actually contracted. In 1962, it traded for around 20 times earnings, but two decades later the market had the stock trading for just 10 times earnings.

But part of it was also Gillette's falling profit margins and falling return on assets:

Date	Profit margin	ROA
12/31/62	16.4%	23.8%
12/31/63	14%	23.2%
12/31/64	12.6%	18.6%
12/31/65	12.5%	19.4%
12/31/66	12.6%	20.6%
12/31/67	13.2%	16.2%
12/31/68	11.3%	15.4%
12/31/69	10.8%	14.7%
12/31/70	9.9%	13%
12/31/71	8.6%	11.2%
12/31/72	8.7%	11%
12/31/73	8.1%	10.7%
12/31/74	7%	8.8%
12/31/75	5.7%	7.8%
12/31/76	5.2%	7.2%
12/31/77	5%	6.7%
12/31/78	5.5%	7.3%
12/31/79	5.6%	7.2%
12/31/80	5.4%	7.3%
12/31/81	5.4%	7%
12/31/82	6%	8%
12/31/83	6.7%	8.6%

In other words, it took more and more sales, and more and more assets, to generate a given dollar of profits. Its return on equity, another important measure, which we'll look at in chapter 6, also fell. It earned 31 percent on every dollar invested in 1962, but by 1982, it earned 18 percent.

Despite its many advantages, Gillette's business was clearly not as good as it was in 1962. There were several reasons for this.

"Gillette had to at times lower the prices of their products in order to compete," Alejandro writes, "just as they did with the Wilkinson stainless

steel blade. Also, R&D costs coupled with the expenses of Gillette's con-
tinuous product launches (both domestically and worldwide) required a
substantial amount of capital."

It was only when Gillette reversed these trends that its real march to
100-baggerdom began in earnest. The valuation bottomed out too. By
the time it became a 100-bagger—from 1964 to the middle of 1995—the
stock's price-to-earnings ratio was a rich 28. Sales and earnings also grew
more rapidly. Sales grew nearly 11 percent annually from 1982 over the
next 15 years. Earnings grew even faster, at nearly a 15 percent clip over
the same period.

And no doubt, a healthier economic environment contributed to the
better performance in the 1980s and 1990s versus the 1970s. Even so,
such things are not predictable, and that is why I (and Phelps and others)
recommend you don't bother to try to be an economic forecaster. I'll have
more to say about this in later chapters.

The Gillette case study reinforces several things we've learned so
far—the importance of growth, for one thing. In this, Gillette was arguably easier to see than Amazon or Comcast. It kept up profit margins and
enjoyed lush returns on both equity and assets.

The Gillette case study also shows how valuation makes a big difference over time as the stock moves from a lower multiple of earnings to a
higher one.

Having said that, you ought to prefer to pay a healthy price for a
fast-growing, high-return business (such as Monster) than a cheap price
for a mediocre business. A little math shows why. Peter Lynch ran through
an example in his book *One Up on Wall Street*:

> All else being equal, a 20 percent grower selling at 20 times earn-
> ings (a p/e of 20) is a much better buy than a 10 percent grower
> selling at 10 times earnings (a p/e of 10). This may sound like an
> esoteric point, but it's important to understand what happens to
> the earnings of the faster growers that propel the stock price.

Here's the math:

	Company A (20% earnings growth rate)	Company B (10% earnings growth rate)
Base Year	$1.00	$1.00
1	$1.20	$1.10
2	$1.44	$1.21
3	$1.73	$1.33
4	$2.07	$1.46
5	$2.49	$1.61
7	$3.58	$1.95
10	$6.19	$2.59

You can see what a radically different place you end up at with the fast grower after 5, 7 and 10 years. If both stocks retain their P/E, company A will end up at $123.80 and will hand you a 5-bagger. Company B will sell for $25.90 and give you a double. Even if the 20-P/E stock fell to 10 P/E, you'd wind up with a lot more money still—a triple.

As Phelps reminds us, "good stocks are seldom without friends." Hence, they are rarely cheap in the usual sense. Don't let a seemingly high initial multiple scare you away from a great stock.

Summary

There is no end to this kind of analysis. We could create a case study for each of the 365 100-baggers. That would make tough reading. So, I won't spend too much time on case studies.

We've done enough with a range of 100-baggers. And we have a basic template emerging, which I'll return to at the end of the book.

Again, I'd like to emphasize that I don't take the statistical approach very seriously here. I am tempted to give more numbers on what a typical 100-bagger looked like. But that would be like giving you the average price of real estate in Columbus, OH. The latter doesn't tell you much because there is residential property, commercial property, industrial property, and so forth. The population is too diverse. The number doesn't mean anything. It's the same with 100-baggers.

For the next few chapters, though, I'd like to explore further the qualities you'll want to look for in these big winners.

CHAPTER 6:

THE KEY TO 100-BAGGERS

If a business earns 18% on capital over 20 or 30 years, even if you pay an expensive looking price, you'll end up with a fine result.

— Charlie Munger

Jason Donville at Donville Kent Asset Management poses an interesting hypothetical.

He says, imagine you invested in a fund 15 years ago whose fund manager delivered the returns shown in the nearby table, "Stellar returns." At first you might think you've found the next Bernie Madoff, who also delivered incredibly steady returns for a long time—by making them up.

But this isn't Madoff. This is real. This manager really exists. His name is Gerry Solloway. And he is the CEO of a Canadian consumer-finance company called Home Capital Group (HCG).

These returns, though, are not returns on a fund. What the table on the next page shows you is the return on equity for Home Capital in each of the 15 years from 1998 through 2012.

ROE is a measure of what return a business generates on the equity invested in the business. Say you invested $100 to start your own shoeshine business. You earn $25 in your first year. Your ROE would be 25 percent.

"Over time," Donville wrote, "the return of a stock and its ROE tend to coincide quite nicely." If you had invested in Home Capital on January 1, 1998, you'd have paid $1.63 per share. In January of 2014, it was about $80 per share. (Today, the shares are worth $98 per share, adjusting for a two-for-one stock split.)

Stellar returns

Year	Annual Return
1998	20.7%
1999	21.8%
2000	23.2%
2001	23.8%
2002	24.3%
2003	27.4%
2004	31.4%
2005	31.8%
2006	27.4%
2007	28.9%
2008	27.8%
2009	28.2%
2010	27.3%
2011	27.1%
2012	25.5%

"Excluding dividends," Donville writes, "the stock is a 49-bagger over the past sixteen years." If you add in dividends, the stock has delivered an annualized return of 28 percent. This is pretty close to Home Capital's ROE.

Donville spends a lot of time looking for companies like Home Capital for his fund. These are companies that consistently earn ROEs of 20 percent or better. It's not the only factor because high-ROE companies can still be lousy investments. Price matters, for example. (Microsoft has always had a great ROE but was a lousy stock for a decade after 2000.)

But once you find a Home Capital, the goal is "to hold this stock or basket of stocks for as long as the company can achieve said returns. Easier said than done, but nonetheless achievable."

Donville writes a quarterly letter called the *ROE Reporter*. He writes about stocks that meet his criteria. These are mostly Canadian companies, as Donville focuses on Canada. His picks for 2014, in the January letter, included Home Capital.

I share the Donville story to make a couple of points. First, it's important to think about what a company can earn on the money it invests. When a company can build book value per share over time at a high clip, that means it has the power to invest at high rates of return.

The second point I want to make is how time is your friend when you own such stocks. In just 16 years, Home Capital multiplied its investors' wealth 49-fold. You could only get that return by holding onto the stock through thick and thin. It was not always smooth sailing. In 2008, to take an extreme, the stock was more than cut in half. Think what a mistake it would have been to sell it!

That's why Donville's focus on ROE is helpful. Just looking at that "Stellar returns" table above, you would not have sold. I have seen similar presentations of ROEs by firms. Remember Phelps's presentation of Pfizer's annual results over a 20-year period? You see steady 15–19 percent ROEs, year in and year out—for twenty years. He asks you, "Would a businessman seeing only those figures have been in and out of the stock?"

Of course, the answer is no. Which begs the question: why do so many investors show an inability to sit still? That's a question you'll have to answer for yourself. People have put forward all kinds of answers. But know this: the only way to make a 49-fold return, or a hundredfold return, is to "buy right and hold on," as Phelps says.

Even lower rates of return pile up impressively. A 15 percent return means an investment doubles in 5 years and quadruples in 10. In 20 years, that pile is more than 14 times larger than it was at the start.

Searching for 100-Baggers in High-ROE Stocks

Jason Donville's Capital Ideas Fund has been a top performer since inception in 2008.

Investing in companies with high and lasting ROEs is the special ingredient that gives his fund such a kick. I called Jason and explained the 100-bagger project and my initial findings. Many 100-baggers enjoyed high ROEs, 15 percent or better in most years.

"That's exactly right, and that's the kind of stuff we look for," he said. We fell into discussing his approach and the magic of great-performing stocks.

Donville found his inspiration in Warren Buffett—a least one version of him. "Buffett makes a style split roughly mid career," Jason said of the Oracle of Omaha. "In the first half of his career, he is a classic Benjamin Graham-style value investor. Undervaluation is defined by short-term accounting metrics— low price-to-book, low price-to-cash flow, low price-earnings."

Then Buffett meets Charlie Munger and he takes on a new definition of value that focuses on stocks that are cheap in relation to the net present value of future cash flows. "In Buffett I," Jason said, "the prediction of future cash flows is not that big a deal because all you're trying to do is buy something really cheap in relation to the current year's balance sheet or the current year's income statement.

"In Buffett II," Jason continued, "he has to have some sense of where earnings are going. And that's why he won't invest in any companies he can't understand, because he can't project earnings."

Those stocks that are most attractive on a net-present-value basis are the ones that can grow at a high rate. And to grow at an above-average rate, they have to have some kind of sustainable competitive advantage. These stocks generate high ROEs.

"And that's where a lot of your 100-baggers come from," Jason said. "I'm not saying they can't come from somewhere else. Other companies will blast away and be 100-baggers, but you can't see them coming in advance. All you can do is look back in awe at this mining stock that had no assets and no profits and see how it went up 100 times. But your and my ability to find the next one are virtually zero."

I agree. In looking over the 100-baggers, I'm finding two broad types: the seemingly random rippers (such as an oil company that hits a gusher) and the more predictable compounders with those high ROEs. Jason prefers the latter.

Let's just say, hypothetically, he said, Dunkin' Donuts went public when it had only 35 locations. We would look at it and say, great concept, great economics, great product and it's only got 35 locations. The United States is a big market. It could have 8,000 locations someday. "That's the kind of stock that could become a 100-bagger over 20 or 30 years," Jason said. "And predictably so. We could look for businesses like that. . . . Smaller, high-ROE businesses where the growth is relatively straightforward."

Jason starts his process by screening the market, looking for high-ROE stocks. "If a company has a high ROE for four or five years in a row—and earned it not with leverage but from high profit margins—that's a great place to start," he said.

But ROE alone does not suffice. Jason looks for another key element that mixes well for creating multibaggers. "The second piece requires some feel and judgment. It is the capital allocation skills of the management team," he said. Here he ran through an example.

Say we have a business with $100 million in equity, and we make a $20 million profit. That's a 20 percent ROE. There is no dividend. If we took that $20 million at the end of the year and just put it in the bank, we'd earn, say, 2 percent interest on that money. But the rest of the business would continue to earn a 20 percent ROE.

"That 20 percent ROE will actually come down to about 17 percent in the first year and then 15 percent as the cash earning a 2 percent return blends in with the business earning a 20 percent return," Jason said. "So when you see a company that has an ROE of 20 percent year after year, somebody is taking the profit at the end of the year and recycling back in the business so that ROE can stay right where it is."

A lot of people don't appreciate how important the ability to reinvest those profits and earn a high ROE is. Jason told me when he talks to management, this is the main thing he wants to talk about: How are you investing the cash the business generates? Forget about your growth profile. Let's talk about your last five acquisitions!

The ROE doesn't have to be a straight line. Jason used the example of Schlumberger, an oil-and-gas-services firm. He'll use what he calls "through-the-cycle ROE." If in an off year ROE is 10 percent, and in a good year it's 30 percent, then that counts as a 20 percent average.

"I'm comfortable buying that kind of stock," Jason said, "and ideally, I'm buying in an off-year."

But he has no interest in companies that lose money in a down cycle. This naturally excludes most mining stocks and many oil and gas stocks, for example.

"The real money to be made in mining stocks and oil and gas stocks is before there are any data for guys like you and me to analyze," Jason told me. "It's those oil and gas stocks that are up 100 times where you go, 'Yeah, but the time when it was a one- or two-bagger, there wasn't anything there for an analyst to dig into.' The only people who got it were the people who bought the lottery ticket from the beginning. And they won. But you can't build a system around picking those kinds of stocks."

By contrast, you could buy a small Panera or a small Chipotle or a small Dunkin' Donuts when they were coming out of the chute. There was enough to analyze. "You could get a really good long run out of some of those quick-service restaurant ideas," he said.

I asked about stock buybacks, which boost ROE. He's agnostic, generally. But he's leery of buybacks and no sales growth. "If you have a company with tons of cash flow but top-line [sales] growth is 5% or less, the stock doesn't go anywhere," he said. "IBM is a good example. Good ROE. Cheap. But the absence of top-line growth means the decline in share count has been offset by multiple contraction." As a result, the stock goes nowhere.

Jason is reluctant to buy a high-ROE company where the top line isn't at least 10 percent. But when he finds a good one, he bets big.

"I started the fund to manage my own money," he told me. "I said to people if you can't pick winners, you should be in exchange-traded funds (ETFs). But if you can pick winners and you put only 1 percent in your best idea, that's irrational."

Jason's fund allows him to put up to 20 percent in any one stock, though he has a self-imposed limit of 12.5 percent. The top five typically make up 50 percent of the fund. These are high-quality companies. "There is no junk in the portfolio," he said. "If one of these guys has a bad quarter, the stock doesn't fall 35%. It falls 3% and then the ROE kicks in, and they are back to normal in no time."

When do you sell, I asked? "If the ROE doesn't fall below 20%, generally, I don't sell," Jason answered, "unless the valuation gets stupid."

And what about insider ownership? He seems to prefer owner-operators, as I do and as our study shows you should—more on that later. "We don't look for it, but we often find it," he said. The guys who make consistently good decisions tend to be owners with skin in the game. They also tend not to take bet-the-company risks.

"The smart entrepreneurs don't actually go for home runs," Jason said. "They hit a ton of singles." He mentioned Constellation Software and MTY Food Group, two of his bigger positions. Management still owns a lot of stock. And it hits lots of singles. The end result is a really nice pattern of growth without risk, he said.

To sum up: It's important to have a company that can reinvest its profits at a high rate (20 percent or better). ROE is a good starting point and decent proxy. I wouldn't be a slave to it or any number, but the concept is important.

You want to think about return on capital in some way—the higher, the better.

You want to think about what a business can earn on the money invested in it and its ability to reinvest cash at that rate—the longer, the better.

The road to 100-baggerdom is much, much harder otherwise.

CHAPTER 7:

OWNER-OPERATORS: SKIN IN THE GAME

My experience as a money manager suggests that entrepreneurial instinct equates with sizable equity ownership. . . . If management and the board have no meaningful stake in the company—at least 10 to 20% of the stock—throw away the proxy and look elsewhere.

— Martin Sosnoff, *Silent Investor, Silent Loser*

Do you remember the Seinfeld episode "The Stock Tip"?

George tries to convince Jerry to go in on a stock with him. There's this guy, Wilkinson. He's made a fortune in the stock market, George says. When Jerry wavers, George says, "C'mon. Wilkinson's got millions invested in this stock."

In the end, the stock works out and George makes $8,000. The episode is funny, but it also reflects a bit of stock market wisdom: bet with the people who have skin in the game.

Here I would like to address a favorite topic of mine and one that applies to 100-baggers: the case of the owner-operator—or, investing with people who own a lot of the stock you're buying.

But first, I want to share a particular quirk in this market of ours that makes the topic of owner-operators timely. For that, I want to turn to some of the work done by the money-management firm Horizon Kinetics.

I listened in on a conference call with Peter Doyle, a money manager at the firm. And we had a good discussion about how the popularity of exchange-traded funds (ETFs) distorts the market. ETFs are essentially ready-made baskets of securities that you buy like a stock. There are real estate ETFs, oil-stock ETFs, gold-stock ETFs, and so on. As people pile into an ETF, that ETF has to go out and replicate its set portfolio—regardless of what the prices of the stocks are.

The people who make these ETFs like to put big, liquid stocks in them. These are easy to buy and sell. The problem is that companies controlled by insiders—thanks to their large stakes—tend not be as liquid as their peers. Thus, the ETFs bypass such companies or give them a low weighting.

As result, Doyle said, "We're finding these owner-operators . . . are being priced well below the marketplace, yet . . . they have returns on capital far in excess of the S&P 500 index or any other index you might be looking at."

It's really an incredible opportunity for the stock picker. You get the better businesses at cheaper prices. Doyle went through a great example to show how dysfunctional things are: Simon Properties.

It's the biggest real estate mall operator in the United States. The stock had gone straight up. It was $26 per share in March 2009. It was $158 per share when Doyle spoke in 2014. The stock yielded 2.9 percent. It traded at more than 30 times earnings.

And the Simon family? They were sellers.

The family dumped over $1 billion worth of stock on the market, which helped the float (or liquidity) of the stock. It was already a big ETF holding. It became an even-bigger ETF holding.

So you have a situation where the stock is expensive and insiders are selling but ETFs are mindlessly buying more. There were other property companies owned by insiders that traded for half (or less) the valuation of Simon with twice the yield. "But because there's not a lot of 'free float,' they're being neglected," Doyle said. "Those are the types of securities that we're looking at and trying to include in most of our funds."

In today's weird marketplace, the presence of owner-operators can be a signal of a likely value. And as with value, an owner-operator is a predictor of future outperformance. "Owner-operators, over an extended period of time," Doyle said, "tend to outpace the broad stock market by a wide margin."

On this topic, there is a wealth of research and practical experience. On the research front, here are a few relevant studies:

- Joel Shulman and Erik Noyes (2012) looked at the historical stock-price performance of companies managed by the world's billionaires. They found these companies outperformed the index by 700 basis points (or 7 percent annually).
- Ruediger Fahlenbrach (2009) looked at founder-led CEOs and found they invested more in research and development than other CEOs and focused on building shareholder value rather than on making value-destroying acquisitions.
- Henry McVey and Jason Draho (2005) looked at companies controlled by families and found they avoided quarterly-earnings guidance. Instead, they focused on long-term value creation and outperformed their peers.

There is much more, but you get the idea. People with their own wealth at risk make better decisions as a group than those who are hired guns. The end result is that shareholders do better with these owner-operated firms. Horizon Kinetics has a neat graphic to illustrate the difference between a typical public company and an owner-operator. (See the chart below.)

The typical public company vs. the owner-operator

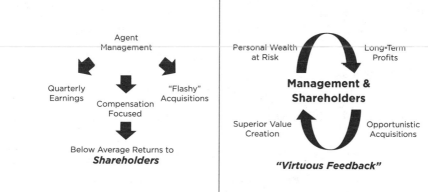

Source: Horizon Kinetics

The Virtus Wealth Masters Fund (VWMCX), managed by Murray Stahl and Matthew Houk, focuses on owner-operator companies. For a stock to get in the fund, management "must maintain a significant vested interest." Stahl and Houk write,

> By virtue of the owner-operator's significant personal capital being at risk, he or she generally enjoys greater freedom of action and an enhanced ability to focus on building long-term business value (e.g., shareholders' equity). The owner-operator's main avenue to personal wealth is derived from the long-term appreciation of common equity shares, not from stock option grants, bonuses or salary increases resulting from meeting short-term financial targets that serve as the incentives for agent-operators.

An example of such a holding is Colfax Corp. (CFX), a maker of a variety of industrial products. The brothers Steven and Mitchell Rales own 24 percent of the stock. They also own 15 percent of Danaher Corp., a similar company. "The return on Danaher shares held over the past 10 years would have been over 3.4 times," the fund managers note, "and well over 59 times if held for 22 years. Colfax is a reprise of Danaher, but at an earlier growth phase."

So my advice again is to stick with the owner-operators.

In the *Seinfeld* episode I mentioned at the outset of the chapter, Jerry sells out in a panic when the stock's price declines, afraid something is wrong. But Wilkinson, the insider, never sold. In the end, George stuck it out with Wilkinson. "I told you not to sell," he tells Jerry. "Wilkinson cleaned up." And so did George.

I called Matt Houk, the co-manager of Virtus Wealth Masters Fund, to discuss the ins and outs of owner-operators in greater detail.

Betting on Billionaires

The sociology of token ownership of equity by both officers and directors of almost all big businesses reinforces an anti-entrepreneurial style that is considered normal behavior, even by the professional investor.

— Martin Sosnoff, *Silent Investor, Silent Loser*

"When my mother asked me what I was doing these days, I explained it to her this way," Matt Houk told me. "I said, 'OK, Mom, what if Warren Buffett approached you and said he'd manage your money [for a small fee]—would you let him?'

"'Of course.'

"'What about Carl Icahn?'

"'Yes.'

"'What about Bill Ackman, David Einhorn or the Tisch family at Loews? Would you let them do it for that fee?'

"'Yes, absolutely.'

"And that's what this fund is. People manage your money for a very reasonable fee and you get access to private equity-type talent.

"Odd that there wasn't a product like this before," Matt explained. "It's such a simple concept. When you put your money in a company, you're entrusting it to that chairperson, that CEO, that board. It would be nice to have them invested alongside you."

That idea is a core part of my own investment philosophy. It also helps in ferreting out 100-baggers. Think of some of the greatest stocks of the last half-century and you often find an owner-operator behind it: Steve Jobs at Apple. Sam Walton at Walmart. Bill Gates at Microsoft. Howard Schultz at Starbucks. Warren Buffett at Berkshire Hathaway. The list goes on and on. These guys are all billionaires.

Here's Matt: "Murray and I were batting ideas around one day and we said, 'Wouldn't it be cool if you could invest in some of these wealth lists like the Forbes 400? I wonder what it would look like.' And that's kind of how we got started."

The Wealth Index was the result and is what the fund seeks to mimic. To get in the index, owner-operators must have assets in excess of $500 million and ownership in excess of $100 million. Applying this filter leaves 148 owner-operators with proven track records. Building this list was not easy—and perhaps that explains the fund's uniqueness.

Usually, people create funds and indices around easily quantifiable data points, such as by price–earnings ratio, or sector or country. These kinds of

things you can easily download from any decent data provider. The Wealth
Index was more difficult to put together.

"It took quite a bit of time," Matt said.

> We were actually in the New York Public Library going through
> microfiche looking for wealthy individuals going back to the early
> '80s. And then every quarter, we took time to comb through SEC
> filings, proxies and Form 4s. It was very manually intensive.

> The operator is very important. In this age of over quantifying ev-
> erything, we lose sight of the fact that it really comes down to the
> people running the business. It's not about the P/E or the historic
> earnings growth necessarily.

Several stocks don't make the index simply because they are too
small. But Matt told me there may soon be an index to capture these
smaller owner-operators.

"We've actually toyed around with the idea of a smaller-cap version of
the Wealth Index to capture those individuals on the up and up, as opposed
to those individuals that have already made it," Matt said. "Something like
a Berkshire Hathaway is appealing. . . . But it is mature. And Warren Buffett
is coming to the end of his career. Are his incentives the same as an Einhorn or an Ackman? No, they're not. So I think a smaller version could
be interesting."

We turned to discussing some of the behaviors of the owner-operators—for example, their penchant for making deals when others are
afraid. Matt elaborated:

> I think this is one of the more important elements of the companies
> in the index. The people running these companies are in control. So
> when we experience a drawdown like 2008, that's precisely when
> they are going to take on more debt and deploy cash. Because the
> opportunities are so rich. That's when you want to be spending
> money. That's when you want to be investing. Compare this behav-
> ior to the agent-operated companies. They loathe spending cash or
> taking on debt in a highly volatile environment. An agent-operator

is so fearful about how that will be perceived by the public and the board and how it may impact his or her career prospects. They just sit there on mountains of cash. And you can see that. There are so many articles out there right now about how companies are hoarding cash at such a high level.

The owner-operators are nothing if not opportunistic. We talked about a few examples, such as Carl Icahn, the famous dealmaker. There are a variety of Icahn-led companies in the index. American Railcar, CVR Energy and Chesapeake are three.

"When you study somebody like Carl Icahn," Matt said, "it becomes very clear that he's using these companies like chess pieces." Let's just look at American Railcar and CVR Energy, for instance. In the oil-rich Bakken, there was a shortage of pipeline capacity to get it to the refineries, such as CVR. One of the only options was to put it on rail cars, and that's what American Railcar makes. "It's interesting to see him play that game," Matt said. "He's now involved in Chesapeake. So there's clearly a strategic element to everything he's doing."

Owner-operators are also tax efficient. Here Matt mentioned John Malone at Liberty Media. "Look at his career," Matt said. "He hates paying taxes. What he tries to do is minimize pretax income, so he can minimize his tax bill. But if you look at Liberty Media, it looks expensive on a price-earnings basis because he's trying to reduce the E. If you approach it from that traditional point of view, you miss the point."

What's also interesting about these owner-operators is they are underrepresented in the S&P 500 index—a widely quoted index meant to stand for the market as a whole. As Matt pointed out, the S&P 500 uses a float-adjusted market cap to determine the weight in the index—meaning, the S&P counts only what is not in the hands of insiders.

"It's the free-float market cap," Matt explained. "So if somebody like Warren Buffett were buying more Berkshire Hathaway, the weighting in the S&P 500 would go down. It's precisely counter to what you would want to happen. If the person running the business were buying more stock, then you want the weight to go up, if anything. The S&P is doing precisely the opposite, which is ridiculous."

Conversely, if an insider sold stock, then its weight in the S&P 500 would go up—again, completely the opposite of what you'd want. Contra the S&P 500, the Wealth Index (and hence the Wealth Masters Fund) is looking for companies with a significant insider.

The proof is in the pudding, as the saying goes. And performance of the index has been top-notch. It's blown the doors off the S&P 500—by about 2.7 percent per year for 20 years. The Wealth Masters Fund is a way for you to invest in this strategy.

There is also academic evidence for the Wealth Index idea.

"When we were getting very close to launching the index," Matt said, "The Journal of Index Investing published a piece titled 'The Rich Get Richer and So Can You: Investing in a Billionaire's Index.' It described our idea very closely. We were startled and thought somebody was going to scoop us. On the other hand, it was nice to see an independent third party validate the concept." (For more on this paper, see the sidebar "Wealth begets wealth.")

We talked about the composition of the index. The highest weight (37 percent) was in consumer discretionary stocks—such as AutoNation, Carnival, Hyatt Hotels or Wendy's. There is hardly any weight in mining, which ought to tell you something. There are many financial and real estate companies. BOK Financial, for example, is a bank run by George Kaiser in Oklahoma. "That's one of the best run banks in history," Matt said. "We're not talking about a Citi or JP Morgan." The insurer W. R. Berkley is another great one. "Greenlight RE—run by Einhorn," Matt added. "That's a financial, but it's really David Einhorn's vehicle."

You can find all the names—a kind of ready-made watch list—by just looking at the fund's holdings, which it discloses publicly.

The index also harbors a variety of insiders and talents: Families that have a long history of creating value—like the Marriott family or the Pritzker family. And investor types—like Nelson Peltz (now involved in Wendy's), John Malone, Icahn, Ackman, Einhorn, Eddie Lampert and others.

"For the average person," Matt summed up, "getting access to investors of that quality is not easy. You can get it only if you go through a hedge fund or a private equity partnership. And you need to be at a high standard of living to qualify. But this is an indirect way to access that talent. And you can have Nelson Peltz invest your money. You can have Carl Icahn and Warren Buffett."

Wealth begets wealth

"Most wealth remains hidden in private financial arrangements undetected by curious onlookers," write Professors Joel Shulman and Erik Noyes. "The public will probably never know the secrets behind this money."

But not all such wealth lies hidden. As we saw with Matt Houk, some of the world's wealthiest own and operate public companies. And we can track how they do—which is what Shulman and Noyes did.

Not surprisingly, they found that, on average, their stocks did well: "We conclude that, overall . . . a portfolio or index of publicly traded stocks represented by the world's wealthiest individuals offers a good deal."

The professors' Billionaires Index—which is very close to the Wealth Masters Index—whooped its peers. As a result, they put forward the idea of buying a basket of such stocks. Again, you can now do this by buying the Wealth Masters Fund.

The professors didn't spend much time thinking about why such companies outperform. But they do give a few clues. One of them is that the rich have access to networks—through social and business connections—that give them better information. It helps them keep their edge over less connected peers.

In my talk with Matt Houk, he mentioned this aspect too. He used Steven Udvar-Házy, the CEO of Air Lease Corp., as an example. Udvar-Házy is the father of the aircraft-leasing business. He has great connections in the business. He can pick up a phone and reach almost anyone. That fact gives Air Lease an advantage.

It's an advantage that doesn't show up in a financial statement or a price–earnings ratio. Yet it is as real as the ground you walk on.

Continue on next page . . .

The professors list many other attributes of success: low costs, modest borrowings, profits throughout economic cycles, low turnover among senior executives and an attention to providing incentives to all stakeholders. "The combined effect," the professors write, "when done well, provides explosive wealth creation for all organization stakeholders."

The exact mix of things may be a mystery, patched together after the fact to explain a result. The most important idea, though, is that the people calling the shots have personal capital at risk. That's the unique attribute that runs through all these stories. That's the secret behind the money.

In the pursuit of 100-baggers, it helps to back talent. Think about finding people who might be the next Jobs, Walton or Icahn. Invest alongside talented people. Many of the best-performing stocks of the past 50 years had such a key figure for at least part of their history. That's the key message of this chapter.

CHAPTER 8:

THE OUTSIDERS: THE BEST CEOS

Many people think of Jack Welch as a great CEO. According to *The Outsiders: Eight Unconventional CEOs and Their Radically Rational Blueprint for Success,* by William Thorndike, if you had invested a dollar with GE when Welch took the helm in 1981, you'd have had $48 when he handed it over to Jeffrey Immelt in 2001. That's a compound return of 20.9 percent, while the overall market delivered 14 percent. GE's total return was 3.3 times that of the market.

That's a pretty darn good record. (I leave aside questions about what happened after he left.) Thorndike uses Welch as a benchmark for great CEO performance. Was Welch the best CEO ever?

Not even close.

Let's look at Thorndike's book, which is an important study of how great CEOs create value. I highly recommend it. The book will make you a better investor. And it serves as a handbook for exactly the kind of thing I spend so much time looking for: truly great owner-operators. Finally, but just as importantly, the quest for the next 100-bagger logically begins with a study of the wizards who have already done it.

Thorndike profiles eight CEOs. Four of their stocks became 100-baggers under their watch. These CEOs include Henry Singleton at Teledyne (180-bagger), Tom Murphy at Capital Cities (204-bagger) and John Malone at TCI (900-bagger). Oh, and Warren Buffett.

There are also four who don't quite make the cut of being a 100-bagger, such as Katharine Graham at the *Washington Post* (89-bagger) and Bill Stiritz at Ralston Purina (52-bagger). But we won't be too doctrinaire about this. With Stiritz, that 52-bagger took just 19 years. Imagine putting $10,000 with him and turning it into $520,000. That can save a retirement.

The point is investing with these people made you a pile of money. You didn't even have to be around for the full ride.

But let's start with the basic thesis of the book.

The main idea is that these CEOs were all great capital allocators, or great investors. Capital allocation equals investment. And CEOs have five basic options, says Thorndike: invest in existing operations, acquire other businesses, pay dividends, pay down debt or buy back stock. (I suppose a sixth option is just sitting on the cash, but that only defers the decision of what to do with it.)

They also have three ways to raise money: issue stock, issue debt or tap the cash flow of the business.

"Think of these options collectively as a tool kit," Thorndike writes. "Over the long term, returns for shareholders will be determined largely by the decisions the CEO makes in choosing which tools to use."

Note what this isn't about. It's not about a "great business." It's not about being in "growing markets." There is no special asset to own. The Outsiders made a fortune in both growing and shrinking markets. They did it in consumer products and media. They did it in financial services and manufacturing. Industry didn't matter.

"None had hot, easily repeatable retail concepts or intellectual property advantages versus their peers," Thorndike writes. "Yet they hugely outperformed them." They did it by using that tool kit to maximum effect. In this, they shared some common thinking.

Each of the Outsiders shared a worldview that "gave them citizenship in a tiny intellectual village." Thorndike writes each understood that

- capital allocation is the CEO's most important job;
- value per share is what counts, not overall size or growth;
- cash flow, not earnings, determines value;
- decentralized organizations release entrepreneurial energies;
- independent thinking is essential to long-term success;
- sometimes the best opportunity is holding your own stock; and
- patience is a virtue with acquisitions, as is occasional boldness.

They shared "old-fashioned, pre-modern values." They were "deeply iconoclastic." Often this was reflected in their geography. New York City does not figure among their chief haunts. Instead, they put themselves outside of the financial nexus.

This helped them ignore the herd, to blot out conventional wisdom and noise. They fostered "simplicity of focus." Outsiders show "a genius for simplicity," Thorndike writes. This allowed them to cut "through the clutter of peer and press chatter to zero in on the core economic characteristics of their business." He provides many examples of all these traits. And you see the result: some jaw-dropping track records.

Take Henry Singleton of Teledyne. (This is one of my favorite case studies in all of business history.) Teledyne was a conglomerate—nothing too special. But look at how Singleton used his tool kit. He avoided paying dividends. He ignored reported earnings, focusing on cash flow. He had Teledyne buy back 90 percent of its stock over time. If you had put $1 with Singleton in 1963, you'd have had $180 when he retired in 1990. He beat the market by a factor of 12.

Singleton and his team were also owners. I cannot stress this enough. When Singleton retired, the board of directors owned 40 percent of the stock. All of the Outsiders' incentives lined up with shareholders'.

Consider another great example: Tom Murphy at Capital Cities. He started out with five TV stations and four radio stations. His competitor, CBS, had 16 times Capital Cities' market cap. Murphy was at the helm of a rowboat against an ocean liner. By the time Murphy was done, Capital

Cities was three times as valuable as CBS. "The rowboat won," Thorndike writes. "Decisively."

Murphy's formula was simplicity itself: Focus on cash flow. Use leverage to acquire more properties. Improve operations. Pay down debt. And repeat. If you had put $1 with Murphy when he became CEO in 1966, you would have had $204 when he sold out to Disney 29 years later. That rate of return's almost 20 percent annually and it beat the market by nearly 17-fold! (And it beat competitors by fourfold.) Under Murphy, Capital Cities bought back 47 percent of its shares.

Another great example from the book is John Malone at TCI, the cable operator. His track record was phenomenal. Every $1 invested in 1973 turned into $900 by 1998. That's 30 percent annually for a long time. Competitors returned 20 percent, while the market overall returned just 14 percent. Malone also bought back 40 percent of the shares outstanding, generating a return of over 40 percent on the repurchases. (I should add that all the Outsiders generated big returns on their repurchases. They knew how to buy low.)

Consider one more example: Bill Stiritz at Ralston Purina. He focused the company on a basic metric: return on equity. To boost it, he used debt. He sold units that did not meet his high hurdles. It all worked brilliantly. One dollar invested with him was worth $57 19 years later. That's a 20 percent annual return, topping peers (17.7 percent) and the market (14.7 percent). He followed many of the principles outlined above. Stiritz also bought back lots of stock, retiring 60 percent of Ralston's shares.

I cannot do justice to the depth of their stories here. Thorndike does an admirable job giving you a concise portrait of the CEOs themselves. You get a sense of their values and where they came from. He also fleshes out how the Outsiders pushed the key principles of their tiny intellectual village that I outlined earlier.

In the end, there is no exact formula. Nonetheless, Thorndike has done us a great service in distilling the essential features of the Outsiders and how they used their tool kit. They "disdained dividends, made disciplined (and occasionally large) acquisitions, used leverage selectively, bought back lots of stock, minimized taxes, ran decentralized organizations and focused on cash flow over reported net income."

The Outsiders did not always do all these things. The right tool from the tool kit varied by circumstance. But all thought like investors and used the tool kit intelligently to make a huge impact in a way conventional CEOs fail to do.

I've already recommended this book to several CEOs and fellow investors. My own copy is full of marked-up pages. I recommend you grab a copy and read it carefully. *The Outsiders* will give you a window into a "radically rational" world. Incredibly, it is one that is still unappreciated by most investors. But it is one that will repay study many times over.

The Next Outsiders

Recently, I got to ask Thorndike about 100-baggers in the making.

In New York, Thorndike sat down for a Q&A moderated by William Cohan, who was an investment banker at Lazard and now writes books and shows up on TV. The New York Society of Security Analysts hosted the event. It was definitely worthwhile.

I won't recount the whole discussion. But I will highlight one part that will interest you. And that is his answer to my question. I asked him what CEOs and companies he thought followed the Outsiders template.

He rolled off several ideas:

- *Nick Howley, TransDigm (TDG)*. Thorndike called TransDigm an "incredible company, based in Cleveland." TransDigm makes highly specialized parts for aircraft. These parts are hard to replace. They are critical to flying aircraft. And there are no substitutes. So TransDigm has a great business. Add in Howley's aggressive buybacks and you have a superpowered stock.

  TransDigm has a cameo in the book, running a couple of pages. If you bought it just after the book came out in October 2012, you'd be up 45 percent. The stock never looks cheap enough to me, but there's no denying it has been a winner. It's up 660 percent since its IPO in 2006.

- *Steven and Mitchell Rales at Danaher (DHR) and Colfax (CFX).* The Rales brothers have been the moving force behind two industrials. Danaher you probably know. It's a giant $58 billion company. The Rales brothers perfected folding in smaller industrials and plugging them into the Danaher machine.

  Colfax is more interesting because it's smaller (only $6 billion market cap) and younger. It went public back in 2008 at $18 per share. The Rales brothers are basically applying the Danaher formula all over again at Colfax. It was on fire for a while. The stock seems to be on sale now, off 30 percent from its high.

- *Mike Pearson, Valeant Pharmaceuticals (VRX).* This one is controversial. There are some vocal critics who think Valeant's business model is all sizzle and no steak. They also dispute the accounting and chafe at the share price. On the other hand, I heard Bill Ackman of Pershing Square cogently defend it at a Grant's Conference. He cited growing cash earnings and the logic of Pearson's deal making.

- *NVR Inc. (NVR).* This is the clear Outsider among homebuilders. Murray Stahl at Horizon-Kinetics wrote about it late in 2013. He summed up its outstanding features:

  > NVR is somewhat of an oddity within the homebuilding industry. It chose not to enter rapidly growing markets such as in California and Arizona, it remained solidly profitable throughout the housing crisis and currently has more cash than debt. This conservative management approach has led the company to also repurchase nearly half of its shares outstanding during the course of the last decade.

  If you ever want to own a homebuilder, you should start with this one.

- *Exxon Mobil (XOM).* Thorndike cited a long, 35-year, track record. It's big and boring. And it feels played out to me. The stock has been a dog for five years. But maybe you can still make good money with it.

- *A whole range of mini-Berkshire insurance companies.* Markel (MKL), White Mountains (WTM) and Fairfax Financial Holdings (FFH on the Toronto Exchange). You probably know these. All follow the same kind of model. They have insurance companies. And they creatively invest the funds to create superior returns over time. It's always an interesting set of names. I watch 'em all. When the market takes another dive, pay attention—that may be the only time you can get any of these on the cheap.

- *Leucadia National (LUK).* As a side note, Thorndike wanted to include Ian Cumming and Joseph Steinberg in the book. The duo headed up Leucadia National, which was a 250-bagger. But the reclusive duo wouldn't cooperate with the author. So Thorndike made the call not to include them, because he thought it was important to meet with every living CEO. He wrote the chapter but didn't publish it.

  Today, Leucadia is a different bug entirely. There was a big merger with Jefferies, the investment bank. Cumming retired. Steinberg remains as chairman. But Rich Handler, top dog at Jefferies, is now also at the helm of Leucadia. Jefferies is a big part of LUK. Basically, don't own LUK unless you like Jefferies. Perhaps the culture of the old Leucadia will carry on. I have my doubts.

- *AutoZone (AZO).* I wrote about AutoZone earlier. It has a great incentive plan. All the incentive metrics—return on capital, earnings per share and total shareholder return—are perfectly aligned with shareholders' interests. No surprise, then, that the CEO is a fan of stock repurchases. AutoZone's share count has declined 75 percent over the past 13 years or so. The compound annual return for shareholders is 21 percent, versus just 3 percent for the market as a whole. (This example runs counter to Donville's objections to IBM and buybacks. We will look at buybacks in more detail in chapter 11.)

Lastly, Thorndike mentioned one that rang a bell, but I couldn't place it at first:

- *Mark Leonard, Constellation Software (CSU:tsx)*. He called it a "small but excellent company in Canada." Then it hit me. I knew where I'd read about this company: in J. P. Donville's *ROE Reporter*. I dug out Donville's note. Here is an excerpt:

  > I am a fan of technology companies, and two companies that we have looked at frequently over the years are Constellation Software and Descartes Systems. Both companies are very successful software companies and thus they each get high marks in terms of making and selling things. But we have chosen to own Constellation Software over Descartes because we think the former is a much better allocator of capital. Constellation's return on equity (as we measure it) is typically three times higher than that of Descartes. . . . Constellation's superior capital allocation strategy has made a significant difference in terms of its long-term share price performance.

  I'll say. Constellation ran from about C$24 per share to C$322 since going public in 2007. That's a 13-bagger. Over the same time, Descartes was a four-bagger.

  Joe Chidley of Canada's *Globe and Mail* wrote a piece about CEO Mark Leonard in April of 2014 ("Constellation Software's Elusive CEO"). He wrote, Leonard "has been favorably compared to Warren Buffett and Prem Watsa [the head of Fairfax Financial]." Leonard also manages a striking level of anonymity for someone with such success in a public company.

  Constellation is a Danaher-like roll-up. It buys a lot of companies, fixes them and reinvests the cash. It made 30 acquisitions in 2013. There is no shortage of targets. The company maintains it has a database of 10,000 acquisition targets.

Leonard is also a big shareholder, with a stake worth over C$400 million. "And he is very protective of shareholders," the *Globe* notes. "Since 2007, Constellation has not issued a single share."

It's an incredible story. Constellation is a worthy Outsider for that second edition.

Ah, but there will be no second edition, Thorndike said. That's too bad. We won't be able to read Thorndike's analysis of the next crop of Outsiders. But we can invest in them.

CHAPTER 9:

SECRETS OF AN 18,000-BAGGER

If people weren't so often wrong, we wouldn't be so rich.

— Charlie Munger at the 2015 Berkshire Hathaway annual meeting

Along with more than 40,000 other people, I was in Omaha, NE, for the Berkshire annual meeting, which also celebrated the 50th anniversary of the company

Here Warren Buffett (age 84) and Charlie Munger (age 91) held court. The two super investors answered questions from the audience and opined on just about everything. Berkshire Hathaway is a must study for any investor, whatever you think of Warren Buffett the man.

The stock has risen more than 18,000-fold, which means $10,000 planted there in 1965 turned into an absurdly high $180 million 50 years later.

How the old buzzard did it is the subject of a minilibrary of books. The latest is *The Warren Buffett Philosophy of Investment*, by Elena Chirkova.

Chirkova's book is notable because she wrote it in Russian and published it in Russia, where it became a bestseller. Chirkova is an associate professor of finance in Moscow.

It's tough to hoe fresh ground in Buffett-land, but she does a great job with one key point most people overlook. And that's Berkshire's use of leverage.

"The amount of leverage in Berkshire's capital structure amounted to 37.5% of total capital on average," Chirkova writes. That would surprise most people.

This leverage came from insurance float. Buffett owned, and still owns, insurance companies. It's a big part of Berkshire's business. As an insurer, you collect premiums upfront and pay claims later. In the interim, you get to invest that money. Any gains you make are yours to keep.

And if your premiums exceed the claims you pay, you keep that too. That's called an underwriting profit.

Everybody knows this part of the story: Buffett invested the float. What people may not know is just how cheap that source of funds was over time. To put it in a thimble: Buffett consistently borrowed money at rates lower than even the US government.

How is that possible? If premiums exceed claims, then Buffett effectively borrowed money at a negative rate of interest. He took in premiums. He invested the money. He kept all the profits. And when he repaid the money (by paying claims), he often paid back less than he borrowed.

From 1965, according to one study, Berkshire had a negative cost of borrowing in 29 out of 47 years. Chirkova cites another study that puts Berkshire's cost of borrowing at an average of 2.2 percent—about three points lower than the yield on Treasury bills over the same period.

This is the key to Berkshire's success. It's hard not to do well when nearly 40 percent of your capital is almost free. This doesn't mean insurance is an easy ticket to riches. Berkshire was smart about what insurance risks it took. That means it had to shrink when the risk and reward got out of whack, which it frequently did (and does).

For example, look at National Indemnity. It is Berkshire's oldest subsidiary. In 1986, NI brought in $366 million in premiums. Then from 1989 to 2000, NI never collected more than $100 million in premiums.

As Chirkova writes,

The decline in revenue over the 1986–1999 period did not occur because business was not obtainable. Berkshire could have collected many billions of dollars in premiums had it been willing to cut prices. However, the company priced its policies to make a profit, not to compete with other insurers. Berkshire never left customers. Customers left Berkshire.

When the opportunity returned, NI stepped in. In 2003 and 2004, it brought in more than $600 million in premiums *each year*.

I cannot emphasize enough how hard it would be for a "normal" insurance company to act this way. Imagine the public shareholders calling for management's heads. "This business hasn't grown for years!"

As Charlie Munger, Berkshire's vice chairman, put it in the last annual letter, "Berkshire's marvelous outcome in insurance was not a natural result. Ordinarily, a casualty insurance business is a producer of mediocre results, even when very well managed. And such results are of little use."

So, summing up here, there are three key points:

1. Buffett used other people's money to get rich.
2. He borrowed that money often at negative rates and, on average, paid rates well below what the US Treasury paid.
3. To pay those low rates required the willingness to step away from the market when the risk and reward got out of whack.

I wonder why more people don't try to emulate Berkshire. It seems, given the success, there should be more firms using insurance float as Buffett did. Most insurers just put their float in bonds. And they try to compete with other insurers on rates.

It's true there is only one Warren Buffett. And it's also true luck plays a role, as it always must. Even Munger admits that Berkshire's success has been so grand that he doubts Buffett himself could recreate it if you gave him his youth back and a smaller base of capital.

Even so, Munger writes, "I believe that versions of the Berkshire system should be tried more often elsewhere."

I do too. An 18,000-bagger is outrageous. It boggles the mind. No one may ever match it. But so what? How about a mere 100-bagger? The template is there.

The Berkshire Hathaways of the Next 20 Years

Now that we have analyzed the gold standard of investing, let's ask, is it possible that other Berkshire Hathaways exist? Let's consider the holding company.

A publicly traded investment holding company is one where the management team has wide freedom to invest as they see fit. They can invest in firms they own in the holding company. Or they can invest in outside firms. They can invest in public entities or private ones. They can even invest in different industries.

The best-in-class example is the aforementioned Warren Buffett's Berkshire Hathaway. It owns publicly traded stocks such as Coca-Cola and IBM. But it also owns companies outright, such as GEICO and See's Candies. It is involved in a mix of industries, everything from insurance to retail.

Berkshire Hathaway is the model investment holding company. It's compounded value by almost 20 percent annually since 1965 (resulting in that 18,000-bagger). There are others, some of which we've mentioned: Leucadia National, Loews Corp., Brookfield Asset Management and Fairfax Financial Holdings. These are the most famous, with long track records of beating the market and compounding money year after year after year—for decades.

You would have been lucky to have put your money with any of them 20 or 30 years ago and left it there. We all know these names now. But what about finding the next generation of great holding companies? What about finding the Berkshire Hathaways of the next 20 or 30 years?

Now, that's an exciting project!

I recently spoke with a money manager, Todd Peters of Lyndhurst Alliance, who has dedicated himself to just such a project. He's already identified 113 candidates. And he's created a portfolio strategy where you can invest alongside him.

I want to share with you notes from my conversation with Todd and from research he shared with me.

"What I'm trying to do now," Todd told me, "is to find the smaller, lesser-known groups that I think have the ability to grow themselves or do deals where we'll look back 30 years from now and see a return pattern similar to Berkshire Hathaway."

He has been studying money managers professionally for two decades in a consulting role. The leaders of holding companies are, essentially, money managers with structural advantages in how they invest. They have permanent capital, unlike, say, a mutual fund manager who must deal with constant inflows and outflows. Holding companies also build businesses, as opposed to just buying and selling stocks. This is what really interests Todd.

He has a passion and enthusiasm for his subject. This is clearly not just a job or a marketing gimmick. He knows the history of holding companies and has studied them with rigor. Todd named his holding-company-focused portfolio the T. F. Ryan Portfolio after financier Thomas Fortune Ryan (1851–1928).

Ryan is widely considered the creator of the first US holding company, the Metropolitan Traction Co. His is a rags-to-riches story. Ryan was born into poverty. By the time he died, though, he was the 10th-richest man in the country, with a fortune estimated at $200 million.

"I spend my free time studying financiers from the 1860s to 1920s," Todd said. When he visits a city, he likes to see whether there is a historic home he can visit to see who created the wealth in that city.

"I started studying these guys when I was in my teens," Todd told me. "I knew about the Vanderbilts, the Rockefellers and Carnegies. But now I'm looking for the second-, third- and fourth-tier ones that aren't as well known. And some of those, to me, are the most incredible stories."

And not all of these stories end well. Some of these people made a bunch of money and also lost a bunch. So you get a ton of lessons out of studying them. Historically, Todd said, there have been five people or groups he considers holding-company inspirations. Ryan was the first, chronologically. The Van Sweringen brothers, from Cleveland, followed him. They at one point owned the most miles of railroad track in the country. They got crushed in the Great Depression, and their holding company eventually became Alleghany—another model holding company today.

Next was Canadian financier Izaak Walton Killam. When he died in
1955, he was Canada's richest man. Fourth were the Bronfman brothers,
who were kicked out of Seagram. Their holding company, Edper, bought
Brascan, which ultimately became Brookfield Asset Management. (In the
'80s, Edper controlled 15 percent of the Toronto Stock Exchange.) And
rounding out the top five is Albert Frère, currently the richest man in
Belgium, who controls the holding company Groupe Bruxelles Lambert.

"Those five groups have been instrumental in how I think about holding companies," Todd said. "And that takes you from the 1880s to today."
He finds the history helpful, as it shows the good holding companies are
business builders.

He notes that wealth creation—real wealth creation, "not flying-first-
class wealth, but having-libraries-named-after-you kind of wealth"—
comes from owning and operating and building businesses and having
a long-term commitment. "And that's what I see in the Brookfields, the
Loews and the Leucadias."

Todd began to build his own list of holding companies in earnest in
2000 when he first came across Albert Frère. The market valued Groupe
Bruxelles Lambert (GBL) based on its public holdings only. But it owned a
25 percent stake in Bertelsmann, the German media company, which was
then private. If that went public, GBL would triple. Because of multiple
holdings, these companies can be complex. They don't fit in easy Wall
Street boxes and largely go unfollowed. This creates opportunities sometimes to buy them cheap.

Intrigued, Todd started looking for more names like Groupe Bruxelles Lambert. Over the years, any time he saw a story or article about
a group or holding company, he would add it to his database. In 2007,
he started to think more seriously about how this idea could work as
a stand-alone investment strategy. By that time, he had about 50 or so
names. Ever since, he's been adding more as he finds them. Now he's up
to 113. The characteristics of this group are interesting.

"I have 18 that are North American, 12 that are in the US," he said at
the time. "The lion's share is outside of the US." He said he wouldn't invest

in the US stocks unless they got hammered. So the T. F. Ryan Portfolio began as an international portfolio out of the gate. Holdings would include Sweden's AB Kinnevik, France's Bolloré Group, Canada's Dundee Corp. and Hong Kong's First Pacific Co.

Todd loves the frontier markets. But he's not ready to have a holding company that's based in, say, Kazakhstan, even though he may believe in its market. Instead, he'd prefer to own holding companies based in developed markets that have businesses in those frontier and emerging markets. This way, at least at the holding-company level, he still gets the benefit of a mature capital market with easily accessible financials, disclosures, and so on.

Todd's investment philosophy is consistent with many of the themes in this book. For example, Todd looks to buy holding companies at a discount to the sum of their parts' value. He also looks for high insider ownership and an owner-operator structure. He prefers fortress balance sheets and low debt levels. These are just a few of the many traits Todd looks for.

As Berkshire Hathaway proves, a holding company structure can reach 100x—and then some.

CHAPTER 10:

KELLY'S HEROES: BET BIG

I can't be involved in 50 or 75 things. That's a Noah's Ark way of investing—you end up with a zoo that way. I like to put meaningful amounts of money in a few things.

— Warren Buffett

Thomas Phelps wrote, "Be not tempted to shoot at anything small," the idea being you want to focus your capital on stocks with the potential to return 100x. You don't want to own a zoo of stocks and ensure a mediocre result.

In this chapter, we explore the idea of concentration in your portfolio.

In Zurich, at the ValueX conference, Matt Peterson of Peterson Capital Management presented the idea of the Kelly criterion. This can get mathematical and wonky, but the basic idea is simple: bet big on your best ideas.

It all began with a man named John L. Kelly Jr. (1923–1965).

Kelly was a Texan, a pilot for the navy in WWII and a PhD in physics. He worked at the storied Bell Labs, where he whipped up what became known as the Kelly criterion in 1956. The story is wonderfully told in William Poundstone's *Fortune's Formula*.

Kelly sought an answer to a question. Let us say a gambler has a tip-off as to how a race will likely go. It is not 100 percent reliable, but it does give him an edge. Assuming he can bet at the same odds as everyone else, how much of his bankroll should he bet?

Kelly's answer reduces to this, the risk taker's version of E = mc²:

$$f = edge/odds$$

F is the percentage of your bankroll you bet. Say you can bet on Big Brown at 5–1 odds at the Kentucky Derby, meaning, if you bet $1, you would stand to win $5 if Big Brown wins. (Plus, you'd get your $1 back.) Odds = 5.

What about your edge? Your inside tip says Big Brown has a one-in-three chance of winning. That means a $1 bet gives you a one-third chance of ending up with $6 ($5 plus your initial $1 bet). On average, such $1 bets are worth $2—for a net profit of $1. Your edge is your profit divided by the size of your wager, in this case, $1. Edge = 1.

Plug it all into the formula, and Kelly says you should bet 20 percent of your bankroll on Big Brown.

If you don't get the math, don't worry about it. The aim of the formula is to find the optimal amount to bet. And the rough answer is this: when you have a good thing, you bet big.

As you might imagine, this is useful for investors because they too face a question: how much do I put in any one stock?

Kelly's formula gives you an objective way to think about it. But it has quirks. For one thing, the formula is greedy. "It perpetually takes risks in order to achieve ever-higher peaks of wealth," as Poundstone writes. It is for making the most the fastest, but that goal is not for everyone.

Yet it is also conservative in that it prevents ruin. It has, as one professor put it, an "automatically built-in . . . airtight survival motive." Even so, it produces large swings in your bankroll. As you can see from our Big Brown example, if you lost—and you would have—you lost 20 percent of your bankroll. This has led some to try to smooth the ride a bit by taking a "half-Kelly." In other words, if the formula says you put 20 percent of your account in one stock, you put half that amount, or 10 percent.

I favor the half-Kelly because it cuts the volatility drastically without sacrificing much return. Poundstone says a 10 percent return using full Kellys turns into 7.5 percent with half-Kellys. But note this: "The full-Kelly bettor stands a one-third chance of halving her bankroll before she doubles it. The half-Kelly better [sic] has only a one-ninth chance of losing half her money before doubling it."

The formula has more ins and outs than I care to tackle here. It set off lots of catfights among academics that raged for decades. (See Poundstone's book for a good look at the debates. Also, Michael Mauboussin has a summary discussion in a 2006 paper titled "Size Matters." You can find it free online.)

For me, the big obstacle is that in the stock market, you can't know your odds or your edge with any certainty. You must guess.

Nonetheless, the idea is alluring. Ed Thorp used it in his hedge fund, Princeton/Newport. Started in 1974, it averaged 19 percent returns for nearly 30 years without a down year. How much of that is due to Kelly's formula and how much to Thorp's own genius is hard to say.

Thorp's example is not a lonely one. Many great investors seem to intuitively use Kelly's formula. Which brings us back to Matt's presentation. He had a fascinating slide, which I reproduce here. (This data was current as of the end of 2014 and relies on public filings. This is not an accurate way to get a read on a portfolio because of certain limitations. For example, investors don't have to disclose foreign-listed stocks and other positions. But it gives you a rough idea of a manager's concentration in disclosed stocks.)

You'll see a number of standout investors and how they bet big on their best ideas. These portfolios look a lot like what Kelly's formula would demand.

Kelly disciples?

Baupost: Seth Klarman
93% of portfolio in 10 positions
14% in Micron Technology (MU)
7% in Cheniere Energy Inc. (LNG)

Hayman: Kyle Bass
6 positions
46% in General Motors (GM)
21% in Nationstar Mortgage (NSM)

ESL Investments: Eddie Lampert
4 positions
55% in Sears Holdings (SHLD)
24% in AutoNation (AN)

Pabrai Funds: Mohnish Pabrai
7 positions
24% in Horsehead (ZINC)
22% in General Motors (GM)

Fairfax: Prem Watsa
98% of portfolio in 10 positions
35% in Resolute Forest (RFP)
31% in Blackberry (BBRY)

Pershing Square: Bill Ackman
7 positions
40% in Allergan (AGN)
20% in Can. Pacific Railway (CP)

Fairholme: Bruce Berkowitz
8 positions
22% in Bank of America (BAC)
13% in Sears Holdings (SHLD)

WL Ross & Co: Wilbur Ross
4 positions
54% in Navigator Holdings (NVGS)
17% in EXCO Resources (XCO)

Now, I doubt any of them is actually going through the trouble of plugging numbers in the edge/odds formula I showed you before. But it is like an analogy I heard once about Minnesota Fats and physics. Fats didn't use math formulas from physics when he lined up a pool shot. But the principles of physics were at work nonetheless. It's just that Minnesota Fats had internalized them through experience.

We might say the same thing for these super investors. The principles of using edge and odds are part of what they do.

Matt's slide showed this in a striking way. To maximize your returns, you're better off following these examples. To flip it around, look at what unsuccessful investors do. The typical mutual fund holds about 100 stocks. None matters very much (or for very long). And most funds are poor mimics of the market.

As Buffett says up top, reject the Noah's Ark way of investing. It seems many great investors do. And it is what I try to do in my own portfolio: Keep the list of names relatively short. And focus on the best ideas. When you hit that 100-bagger, you want it to matter.

CHAPTER 11:

STOCK BUYBACKS: ACCELERATE RETURNS

What is a "tontine"?

If you think a tontine is a rich French pastry, you're half right. It is indeed French. But a tontine is not a pastry.

It is, instead, a tactic for amassing riches that is both legal and non-fattening. But first, I'd like to tell you about a guy named Lorenzo Tonti, from whom the word—tontine—derives.

Imagine the scene. The year is 1652. The place: France, during the reign of the House of Bourbon. King Louis XIV broods on his throne. The French treasury is bare.

Meanwhile, there is an ongoing war with Spain, and he needs money to continue it.

He invites Lorenzo de Tonti, a banker from Naples, to his decadent court. Tonti has an idea.

"Let us have citizens invest in shares of a government-run pool," Tonti suggests. "We will pay regular dividends to them from the pool. But they cannot transfer or sell their shares. And when they die, they lose their shares. We cancel them." Tonti's eyes narrow, and he tugs thoughtfully at one of his whiskers.

"Yet," Tonti continues with eyebrows arched, "we promise to pay the same amount regardless of how many shares remain. So as each shareholder dies, the remaining shareholders get more and more of the earnings of the pool. That reward will prove a great pull for investors and will raise the funds you seek."

The king stirs.

"When the last shareholder dies"—Tonti winds it up—"the capital of the pool reverts to the state." The king, with a wolfish grin, rubs his hands together greedily. Tonti's plan would serve his purpose. Yet upon reflection, even the dense king could see that the big winners of this scheme would be the long-lived holders of the shares. They would earn an increasing share of the dividends as others died off and would grow rich.

He did not pursue Tonti's idea, but others would.

I think Lorenzo de Tonti would be amused to see the modern twist on his idea.

(There is some skepticism that Tonti actually invented the idea. Some evidence suggests it was an older Italian scheme that Tonti simply took to the effete French court.)

Today, Tonti would be an activist getting in front of CEOs, not kings, speaking of the wonders of retiring shares. And more than a few 100-baggers greedily bought back their own shares when the market let them do so cheaply.

Stock Buybacks: Modern Tontines

Stock buybacks deserve a separate chapter in a book on 100-baggers because they can act as an accelerant when done properly.

A buyback is when a company buys back its own stock. As a company buys back shares, its future earnings, dividends and assets concentrate in the hands of an ever-shrinking shareholder base.

Many companies are doing buybacks these days. In a slow- to no-growth economy, this tactic is becoming a more important driver of earnings-per-share growth.

But you have to actually shrink the number of shares outstanding.

Since 1998, the 500 largest US companies have bought back about one-quarter of their shares in dollar value, yet the actual shares outstanding grew. This is because they hand out the shares in lavish incentive packages to greedy executives.

But don't let the bad examples take away from the wisdom of the concept. There are some companies that exemplify the very best of the practice.

One example is AutoNation—a classic I mentioned before. Eddie Lampert took a stake in 2000. Lampert, a great investor, knows how tontines work. Ever since his involvement, AutoNation has bought back gobs of stock. All told, 65 percent of the shares have been retired.

That's 8.4 percent per year—just from stock buybacks. As Steve Bregman at Horizon-Kinetics, which owns a 5 percent stake in AN, writes, "This is most unusual in scale and duration; one is witnessing—or may participate in—a slow going-private transaction that is taking place in the open market."

The effects have been wonderful for the stock. AutoNation is up 520 percent since the tontine began. Annualized, that's better than 15 percent per year—for 13 years! The chart above shows you the last 10 years. You can see the fall in shares outstanding and the surge in the stock price.

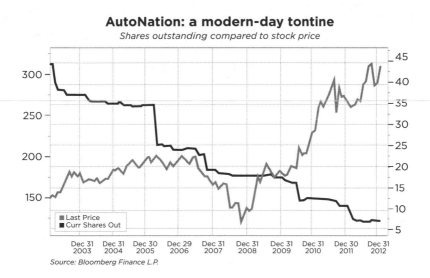

AutoNation: a modern-day tontine
Shares outstanding compared to stock price

Source: Bloomberg Finance L.P.

Meanwhile, Lampert held onto his shares and his stake swelled. He's trimmed it a bit in the last couple of years but still owns almost 53 percent of the stock.

An even-longer-term example is Loews Corp. I admire the skills and patience of the Tisch family, which controls Loews. The family is also the largest shareholder. Loews has consistently bought back stock. Over the past four decades, Loews cut the total number of shares outstanding by more than 70 percent. This has helped returns immensely. Every dollar invested in Loews in 1961 is worth about $1,240 today.

In a way, these companies become more valuable by losing shareholders. It sounds strange, but in essence, this is what's happening. The victors are those who simply hold on.

The practice is abused and more widespread than it should be. As Warren Buffett puts it in his 2000 letter to shareholders,

> There is only one combination of facts that makes it advisable for a company to repurchase its shares: First, the company has available funds—cash plus sensible borrowing capacity—beyond the near-term needs of the business and, second, finds its stock selling in the market below its intrinsic value, conservatively calculated.

If those two requirements are met, Buffett is an enthusiastic supporter of stock buybacks. This is from his 1980 letter to shareholders:

> We can't resist pausing here for a short commercial. One usage of retained earnings we often greet with special enthusiasm when practiced by companies in which we have an investment interest is repurchase of their own shares. The reasoning is simple: *if a fine business is selling in the marketplace for far less than intrinsic value, what more certain or more profitable utilization of capital can there be than significant enlargement of the interests of all owners at that bargain price?* The competitive nature of corporate acquisition activity almost guarantees the payment of a full—frequently more than full price—when a company buys the entire ownership of another enterprise. But the auction nature of security markets often allows

finely-run companies the opportunity to purchase portions of their own businesses at a price under 50% of that needed to acquire the same earning power through the negotiated acquisition of another enterprise. (emphasis added)

When done right, buybacks can accelerate the compounding of returns.

Stock buybacks have only become more common in the last couple of decades. Therefore, in my study of 100-baggers—which spans 1962 to 2014—it was not a common tactic. But those who were diligent buyers of their own stock had spectacular results, as we saw in chapter 8 with the Outsiders.

It's a potential clue. When you find a company that drives its shares outstanding lower over time and seems to have a knack for buying at good prices, you should take a deeper look. You may have found a candidate for a 100-bagger.

CHAPTER 12:

KEEP COMPETITORS OUT

A truly great business must have an enduring "moat" that protects excellent returns on invested capital.

— Warren Buffett

In the overwhelming number of cases, a company needs to do something well for a very long time if it is to become a 100-bagger. Persistence is as essential to a 100-bagger as gin to a martini.

So, what signs can we look for in a business that it has what it takes to run for 20 years?

This gets us to the topic of moats.

A moat is what protects a business from its competitors. It is a durable competitive advantage. (Phelps called it a "gate"—same idea.) Warren Buffett popularized the idea, and the literature on this topic is vast. I will highlight a few things here, including an unpublished study by Matthew Berry, Columbia Business School alumnus and formerly of Lane Five Capital, that gives a definitive answer—or at least, the most definitive I've seen yet.

When I think of moats, I think of Pat Dorsey. He was the director of equity research at Morningstar and is currently the president of Sanibel Captiva Investment Advisers. Dorsey writes and speaks extensively on moats.

In his *The Little Book That Builds Wealth*, Dorsey uses an analogy for why you should pay attention to moats: "It's common sense to pay more for something that is more durable. From kitchen appliances to cars to houses, items that last longer are typically able to command higher prices. . . . The same concept applies in the stock market."

Companies that are more durable are more valuable. And moats make companies durable by keeping competitors out. A company with a moat can sustain high returns for longer than one without. That also means it can reinvest those profits at higher rates than competitors. As you've seen by now, this is an important part of the 100-bagger recipe.

Moats take various forms. Here are some:

- *You have a strong brand.* Tiffany's has a moat. People pay up just to get that blue box, even though what is in the box might be had somewhere else for less. Oreo is a brand. It may not allow for premium prices, but it inspires loyalty and ensures recurring customers. That's a moat.

- *It costs a lot to switch.* Dorsey has a great example where he talks about banks. There is not much of a competitive advantage that one bank can have over any other. They all have the same products. And with the Internet, branch locations are not even very important. Yet when you look at the numbers, people tend to stay at their banks for six to seven years. The reason is it's a pain in the neck to change banks. As economists say, "switching costs" are high. That's a moat.

- *You enjoy network effects.* Microsoft had a great moat for years. Everybody used its operating system. And so you wanted to use its operating system too. The more people who use these products, the more they enjoy network effects. Think of Twitter, Facebook and YouTube. It's very hard for competitors to crack a network moat. It's like trying to sell the first telephone.

- *You do something cheaper than everybody else.* If you are the low-cost guy, like Walmart, you have a moat. Interactive Brokers is cheaper than every other discount broker, and it's not even close. And that partly explains why it's growing twice as fast as its competitors. That's a moat.

- *You are the biggest.* This gets to some inherent advantages of size. Absolute bigness can be an advantage if it keeps competitors out. Imagine what it would take to try to replicate an Intel or Walmart. But relative size can also be a moat. If you are the dominant insurer of small taxi fleets, as Atlas Financial is, then you have a moat. Competitors are unlikely to invest the time and energy necessary to compete in what is a niche market.

The aforementioned Berry made an interesting point here about the size of the firm relative to the market: "Imagine a market where the fixed costs are high, and prices are low. Imagine that prices are so low that you need 55% of the market just to break even. How many competitors will that market support? One. Not two, not three . . . one."

The firm that gets that 55 percent is in a commanding position. It can keep prices just high enough that it can keep others out and earn a good return. "What matters is the amount of the market you need to capture to make it hard for others to compete," Berry points out.

This is not meant to be an exhaustive look at moats. There are many other ways, some subtle, in which a company could create a barrier other companies have trouble breaking through.

In any event, it is easier to talk about these in the abstract than it is to find them, definitively, in real life. It's easy to talk yourself into why, say, Coach has a moat. But does it really have a moat? Also, competitors have a way of eventually finding a way across many supposed moats.

A great product alone is not a moat. Dorsey uses the example of the Chrysler minivan, which was the first minivan and sold well. But soon after, competitors had their own minivans. Chrysler could not charge more for its minivan. There was no reason to get a Chrysler minivan over any other. It had no moat.

Sometimes this gets tricky. In his book, Dorsey uses Krispy Kreme as a company with no moat. It makes a great doughnut, but it's easy to switch and Krispy Kreme can't charge premium prices for its doughnuts. But some people do love Krispy Kreme doughnuts—including me—and, given a choice, would go for KK over Dunkin Donuts. I'm not so sure it has no moat. See what I mean about how moats can be hard to identify definitively?

On the other hand, most people believe Coca-Cola has a moat, even though there are many other things to drink. Coke's best customers won't settle for anything less than a Coke when they want it. Coke's brand is known all over the world. Coke products are in nearly every corner of the globe. Coke does have a moat (or perhaps "did," as there is evidence that Coke may be losing its moat).

Chipotle is a quick-service restaurant chain that went from 0 stores to 500 in 13 years. It makes fresh Mexican food. As investor Mohnish Pabrai wrote, "Chipotle has a durable moat. This durable moat causes customers like me to continue to go there regardless of the wait. This moat allows Chipotle to have the ability to earn supernormal profits."

"Supernormal profits" is an interesting phrase. It gets more to the heart of what a moat is all about and why it matters.

Great management by itself is not a moat, a point Dorsey makes as well. You have surely heard the quip from Warren Buffett that "when management with the reputation for brilliance meets a company with a reputation for bad economics, it's the reputation of the company that remains intact." Remember it, because it's true.

Moats are also, as I've hinted, not permanent. Competitors eventually figure out their way across. In Pabrai's book *The Dhandho Investor*, he cites Delta, Gateway and General Motors as all having had deep moats at one time. None of them do now. One of the reasons is management teams can also make mistakes and destroy brands. New Coke didn't go over so well. And as we saw in an earlier chapter, corporate lifespans continue to shrink.

Mauboussin on Moats

Michael Mauboussin, a strategist at Credit Suisse, has also done some good work on moats. "Measuring the Moat: Assessing the Magnitude and Sustainability of Value Creation" is a 70-page report on the issue. (You can find it free online.)

Mauboussin looked at 68 global industries, with a sample size of over 5,500 companies. And what he found was that some industries are better at creating value than others. The airline industry, for example, is a terrible industry. Paper and forestry products tend to be a weak industry. He doesn't mention it, but gold mining is another that is notorious for poor returns on capital.

But there are also industries that are pretty good. Communications equipment is one. Within these industries, though, you have winners and losers. As Mauboussin observes,

> The central observation is that even the best industries include companies that destroy value and the worst industries have companies that create value. That some companies buck the economics of their industry provides insight into the potential sources of economic performance. Industry is not destiny.

This is useful to know because some investors will avoid industries entirely—like airlines—that have been bad for investors. But there are many ways to make money within the airline industry.

Mauboussin suggests creating an industry map. This details all the players that touch an industry. For airlines this would include aircraft lessors (such as Air Lease), manufacturers (Boeing), parts suppliers (B/E Aerospace) and more. This is beyond the scope of what an individual investor would do, but even though you aren't likely to make your own industry map, it's a useful mental model.

What Mauboussin aims to do is show where the profit in an industry winds up. These profit pools can guide you on where you might focus your energies. For example, aircraft lessors make good returns; travel agents and freight forwarders make even-better returns.

Mauboussin's industry analysis also shows that industry stability is another factor in determining the durability of a moat. "Generally speaking," he writes, "stable industries are more conducive to sustainable value creation. Unstable industries present substantial competitive challenges and opportunities."

The beverage industry is a stable industry. Trends there unfold slowly over time. Sodas don't get disintermediated by the Internet. Smartphones, by contrast, constitute a very unstable market. BlackBerry smartphones went from market leader to also-ran status in a few years. Since 100-baggers need time to ripen, Mauboussin's research indicates you may be better served in industries less susceptible to sweeping changes in the competitive landscape.

Further, we're always up against the shortening lifespans of companies. Mauboussin writes,

> Research by Credit Suisse HOLT® shows that less than 50 percent of public firms survive beyond ten years. Our analysis of the BDS data also reveals low survival rates. Exhibit 15 shows one-year and five-year survival rates based on the birth year of the establishment. The rate today is similar to that of 1977. The latest figures show one-year survival rates of about 75 percent and five-year survival rates of roughly 45 percent.

All the more reason finding a good moat is important.

So that's the gist of the theory and experience on moats. There's a lot more I could say about it. As investors, we can think about these things in an abstract way. But one analyst found empirical evidence that we might want to favor a certain type of company.

Overcoming Mean Reversion

Moats, in essence, are a way for companies to fight mean reversion, which is like a strong current in markets that pulls everything toward average. If you earn outsized returns, mean reversion says over time your returns will fall toward the average (or mean) over time. If you earn low returns, mean reversion says over time your returns will likely rise to average.

Mean reversion reflects the competitive nature of markets, the fact that people are always reacting and anticipating and working to make more money. There's a lot of natural shuffling going on as people create new products and new businesses and shut down old ones. Capital sloshes around, funding promising ventures and draining less attractive ones. The whole competitive mosaic is always changing.

Anyway, we don't have to explain why exactly mean reversion happens. The fact is we see it in the numbers.

Here we turn to the aforementioned Matthew Berry and his unpublished paper "Mean Reversion in Corporate Returns." His study covers the 15 years from 1990 to 2004. It includes the 4,000 largest companies primarily located in the United States, the UK, Canada, Germany, France, Italy and Spain.

"Mean reversion is a well-documented phenomenon," he writes. "Mean reversion is driven by the trending of returns, on average but not exclusively, towards the mean. Some companies persist as high performers, others as low performers, while a few even change places."

Ah, here we have something interesting. Mean reversion does not affect all companies equally. What might those that persist as high performers have in common?

By "high performers," Berry means those companies that continue to earn a high return on invested capital (ROIC). He's looking at a company's pretax profit over its average capital. He also breaks this down to look at the various drivers of ROIC, such as growth, margins and more.

While many of the variables are quite volatile and do mean revert, Berry found that gross profit margins "are surprisingly resilient and do not contribute meaningfully to fade rates."

Berry runs through a variety of tests. But I will just present the main finding here. Berry writes that "high gross margins are the most important single factor of long run performance. The resilience of gross margins pegs companies to a level of performance. Scale and track record also stand out as useful indicators."

That part about pegging means that if a company started with a high gross profit margin, it tended to keep it. Conversely, when it started off with a low gross profit margin, it tended to stay there as well. Gross margins persist, to use the statistical lingo.

Berry thinks gross margin is a good indication of the price people are willing to pay relative to the input costs required to provide the good. It's a measure of value added for the customer. Not every company shows a huge gross margin. "Amazon's are pretty mediocre," Berry pointed out in an email to me, "but it is clear that the value added is in the selection and the convenience, not in the good itself (which could be found anywhere). But if you can't see how or where a company adds value for customers in its business model, then you can be pretty sure that it won't be a 100-bagger. Unless it strikes oil!"

There are other wrinkles to Berry's research that add to this insight. First, know that the difference between a gross profit margin and an operating profit margin is expenses often dubbed SG&A—for selling, general and administrative—overhead, in other words.

These operating expenses are volatile. When an underperformer improves, this is often an area where you see the improvement. Put another way, if gross margins are sticky and persistent, then a good turnaround candidate would be one with a high gross profit margin and a low operating margin. The latter is easier to fix than the former.

And bigger companies tend to cement their advantages. "Larger companies appear able to sustain returns for longer by finding efficiencies in SG&A that small companies cannot," Berry writes.

Finally, a track record of high performance is a useful indicator. Winners tend to remain winners. This makes sense, since high performance usually comes from some competitive advantage. And these advantages do not tend to "disappear overnight."

I can hardly do justice to Berry's robust paper and its many facets. I will simply try to draw a conclusion on moats that will be useful in hunting for 100-baggers.

I'd sum up this way: It is great to have a moat, but true moats are rare and not so easy to identify all the time. Therefore, you should look for clear signs of moats in a business—if it's not clear, you probably are talking yourself into it— you may also want to find evidence of that moat in a firm's financial statements. Specifically, the higher the gross margin relative to the competition, the better.

CHAPTER 13:

MISCELLANEOUS MENTATION ON 100-BAGGERS

Definition: men·ta·tion (men- t -sh n/) noun. technical. 1. mental activity.

In James Thurber's *Let Your Mind Alone!*, there is a chapter called "Miscellaneous Mentation" that speaks precisely to what this chapter is all about. He writes,

> In going back over the well-thumbed pages of my library of recent books on mental technique, I have come upon a number of provocative passages which I marked with a pencil but, for one reason or another, was unable to fit into any of my preceding chapters. I have decided to take up this group of miscellaneous matters here, treating the various passages in the order in which I come to them.

And so this chapter too is "miscellaneous mentation" on 100-baggers. It doesn't seem to fit anywhere else and so it goes here—in no particular order of importance. One of the things I admire about Phelps's book is the way he packs in so much investing wisdom gleaned from a variety of sources and experiences.

It seems to me a book on 100-baggers must be like this because much of the hunt is qualitative, not driven by any formula. Moreover, realizing a 100-bagger return means you must adopt a certain mindset.

Looking for 100-baggers means you're not going to care much about what the Federal Reserve is doing. It means you're not going to buy a stock because you like the chart (next month's chart might give us a whole different signal). Paying attention to these things is a distraction. Investing for 100-baggers means you have to plant your feet firmly in the ground and stand still.

In this chapter, I have a variety of investing ideas that will help you adopt the needed 100-bagger mindset.

Don't Chase Returns

The year 2014 was one of the worst ever for stock pickers. But almost everyone thinks about this in the wrong way. And it could cost you a lot of money in the long run if you think this way too—especially if you let it distract you from your pursuit of 100-baggers.

First, here's some evidence from near the end of that year:

- Bank of America Merrill Lynch research shows fewer than 20 percent of active managers were ahead of the market that year, the worst performance of more than a decade.
- Bill Alpert, at *Barron's*, says, "Less than 15% of the money managers who actively select stocks are ahead of their benchmarks."
- Denys Glushkov, a researcher at Penn, says only 9.3 percent of all mutual funds that invest in big US stocks such as those in the S&P 500 were ahead of the index through September 30. The previous low was 12.9 percent in 1995 and the average over the previous quarter-century is 38.6 percent.

Glushkov says that 2014 "is likely to enter the record books" as the year when active managers—as opposed to index funds—"delivered their worst performance relative to the index, net of fees, since at least 1989."

And they did.

Faced with that experience, people poured money into passive funds—such as S&P index funds. As nearly everyone knows, the universe of stock pickers can't beat the market because of fees. Still, this year was an epic rout.

There's been a lot of ink spilled about why this is. I don't really care about these scribblings because we're all guessing. But secondly, even if we knew, it doesn't mean we'd be able to predict when things would change.

So, here's part one of my advice: don't try to chase returns, because doing so will cost you a lot of money over time.

Most people won't do that. Most people chase returns. As an example, consider one of my favorite studies of all time, by Dalbar. It showed that the average mutual fund earned a return of 13.8 percent per year over the length of the study. Yet the average investor in those funds earned just 7 percent. Why?

Because they took their money out after funds did poorly and put it back in after they had done well. Investors were constantly chasing returns.

A favorite example of mine is Ken Heebner's CGM Focus Fund. It was the best fund of the decade ending 2010. Heebner's fund turned in a sparkling 18 percent annualized return. Yet the typical investor in his fund earned just 11 percent. It's the same thing: people pulled money out when he had an off year and plowed back in after he had a great year.

I wrote about this in my first book, *Invest like a Dealmaker*. And the advice I gave there is still the advice I give today. To illustrate that advice, let's look at how Mohnish Pabrai answered a question put to him by *Barron's*.

Pabrai's fund has returned close to 10 percent annualized over the last 10 years, beating the S&P index by about 1.5 percentage points. But he's well behind the index this year. Here's *Barron's*:

> When asked about this underperformance, he replied, "*I think it is an irrelevant data point. There is nothing intelligent that one can say about short periods like 10 months. I never make investments with any thought to what will happen in a few months or even a year.*" (emphasis added)

The problem with the 24/7 media culture we live in is that everybody has to have something to say almost all the time. And yet most of the time there really isn't anything worth saying.

So, we get incessant daily commentary on every blip in stocks, gold, bonds and so forth. It's all meaningless drivel. I'm with Pabrai: there really isn't anything intelligent to say about returns over such a short period of time.

In fact, I'll go further: I don't think you should compare yourself to the S&P 500, or the broader market, at all.

Here's what Martin Whitman, one of my favorite investors, has to say about it:

> Certain economists believe strongly that the goal of profession-al money managers is to beat the market. If professional money managers fail to beat the market either individually or en masse, this is taken as evidence that they are useless. . . . The kindest word we have for this point of view is that it is amateurish. (emphasis added)

This is from *Modern Security Analysis* by Whitman and Fernando Diz. I love Whitman's approach, and Whitman has had a big influence on how I think about investing over the years.

The reason Whitman has such disdain for the market-beating point of view is that managers have different goals and duties. A manager invest-ing for an endowment may aim for safety and income over capital gains. Thus, if such a manager turned in a 9 percent return with a portfolio of conservative names that never missed a dividend, it seems silly to rip him for trailing the S&P.

Besides, who cares about one year?

You have to play the long game. There are approaches and investors who have beaten the market by a solid margin over time. The thing is, they seldom beat the market consistently.

The best investors lag the market 30–40 percent of the time. As Bar-ton Biggs once wrote after analyzing the stellar returns of superstar in-vestors, "None in the group always beat the S&P 500 probably because no one thought that was the primary objective."

As I say, there are ways to beat the market over time. But none of these approaches always beats the market. Even the best lag it, and often. As an individual, though, you have a great advantage in that you can ignore the benchmark chasing.

Keep that in mind before you reshuffle your portfolio after looking at year-end results. Don't chase returns! And don't measure yourself against the S&P 500 or any other benchmark. Just focus on trying to buy right and hold on.

Don't Get Bored

People are dying of boredom.

— Raoul Vaneigem, *The Revolution of Everyday Life*

I was at lunch with a friend of mine and we were talking about the big vote in Scotland on whether it should be independent of the UK. (Its citizens chose to stay.)

Then my friend offered up a reason why many people would vote yes: "They're bored! They just want something to happen."

The more I thought about this, the more I thought there might be something to it. Boredom can explain a lot. It can explain all kinds of financial behavior. And there is definitely a "boredom arbitrage" to take advantage of in the markets.

Below, then, is a tongue-in-cheek exploration of my theory of boredom.

Let's start at the beginning: boredom was invented in 1768—well, not the concept, but the word "bore" first appeared in the English language in print in that year. So says my copy of the *Oxford English Dictionary*. (And yes, I have the physical copy—all 20 volumes!) The OED defines the word "bore" in this way: "to be weary by tedious conversation or simply by the failure to be interesting."

Funnily enough, the first usage appeared in a letter by an Englishman complaining about the French to a fellow Englishman: "I pity my Newmarket friends who are to be bored by these Frenchmen."

"Boredom"—as in "the state of being bored"—came along much later. In 1852, Dickens used it in Bleak House: "the malady of boredom."

Author Tom Hodgkinson would agree with Dickens. In his *The Freedom Manifesto*, he has a whole chapter devoted to boredom. He writes, "If contemporary science were more sophisticated and subtle, then I'm absolutely certain that it would rank boredom as one of the central killers in the modern world. . . . It would not surprise me one jot if boredom were one day revealed to be a carcinogenic."

Read in the proper, light-hearted spirit, Hodgkinson's book is terrific. He talks about all the ways in which modern life creates boredom—especially in the workplace.

There are many mechanical, boring jobs that "require just enough concentration to prevent you from going off into a dream but not enough really to occupy your mind." As a result, we have boredom on a mass scale. People are bored. And they do all kinds of things to alleviate the boredom. They act like idiots. They dress like fools. Anything to kill the boredom. They may even commit acts of sabotage.

In the financial markets, people often wind up sabotaging their own portfolios out of sheer boredom. Why else put money into tiny 70-cent-share mining companies that have virtually no chance of being anything at all? Why bother chasing hyped-up biotech companies that trade at absurd levels based on flimsy prospects?

Because people are bored!

It seems exciting to lose your money in this way. It's no different from going to a casino. (And just like a casino, these bets pay off often enough to keep people coming back.) People crave the action.

Why do people buy and sell stocks so frequently? Why can't they just buy a stock and hold it for at least a couple of years? (Most don't.) Why can't people follow the more time-tested ways to wealth? I'm sure you can guess my answer by now.

People often do dumb things with their portfolio just because they're bored. They feel they have to do something. (Here I recall that bit of wisdom from Pascal that "all men's miseries derive from not being able to sit in a quiet room alone.")

I know I get bored, but in a different way. For example, it's incredible to me that people spend so much time talking about the Federal Reserve. My newsletter peers, people in the media—they all do it. It's unbelievable. Don't these people get bored? Or do they do this because they're bored?

I'm so bored with the Federal Reserve. Boring. And, thankfully, it is largely irrelevant to you as an investor. Warren Buffett himself once said, "If Fed Chairman Alan Greenspan were to whisper to me what his monetary policy was going to be over the next two years, it wouldn't change one thing I do."

I read every day somebody, somewhere writing about QE or interest rates or the dollar. They are mostly rehashing the same old narrative: "When QE stops, stocks will fall." "The dollar is going to collapse!" "When interest rates go up, stocks will fall." I mean, for crying out loud, how much more can you read about this stuff? And for how many years on end?

It's just the same old pot of beans, heated up and re-served again and again and again.

This is part of the reason why I travel. That way I don't have to write about what the Fed said this week, or go over some garbled macro scenario I drew up in my head. Instead I can write about what I see—in Greece, hopefully overlooking stunning cliffs and deep blue water. Or in Germany, sitting at a long wooden table under oak trees drinking beer at a thousand-year-old brewery. Not boring!

But seriously, at least it actually has something to do with the real world. As an investment writer, I'm almost desperate to find something new, something different, something *interesting* to write about. You don't need me to repeat what is in the newspapers. You don't need me to add to the cacophony of noise you already hear.

In fact, taking advantage of the noise is a simple arbitrage. Sometimes you'll hear (smart) people talk about "time arbitrage." The idea is just that most investors have a hard time looking out even just a year or two. They focus on now. And so, the idea goes, all you have to do is think out a year and you can pick up stocks that are cheap today because others can't look beyond the current quarter or two or three.

The same kind of arbitrage exists with boredom. People get bored holding the same stock for a long time—especially if it doesn't do much. They see other shiny stocks zipping by them, and they can't stand it. So they chase whatever is moving and get into trouble.

As the famed money manager Ralph Wanger used to say, investors tend to like to "buy more lobsters as the price goes up." Weird, since you probably don't exhibit this behavior elsewhere. You usually look for a deal when it comes to gasoline or washing machines or cars. And you don't sell your house or golf clubs or sneakers because someone offers less than what you paid.

Speaking of Wanger, he wrote an investment book called *A Zebra in Lion Country*, published in 1997. It's an entertaining read and I recommend it. In it, he gets at the boredom arbitrage: "Usually the market pays what you might call an entertainment tax, a premium, for stocks with an exciting story. So boring stocks sell at a discount. Buy enough of them and you can cover your losses in high tech."

That was in 1997, before the bubble popped in 2000. Good advice from Wanger, as usual. (I met him once in his office in Chicago in 2005. He was generous with his time and spent almost two hours with me, just sharing his wisdom.) Today, the market seems bored with just about anything that isn't tech, biotech, social media or Tesla.

Anyway, if you can find ways to fight boredom and not take it out on your portfolio, your returns will benefit.

Just keep your eye on the prize: hundredfold returns are not boring.

Don't Get Snookered: Avoid Scams

But when a man suspects any wrong, it sometimes happens that if he be already involved in the matter, he insensibly strives to cover up his suspicions even from himself. And much this way it was with me. I said nothing and tried to think nothing.

—Herman Melville, *Moby Dick*

I heard Carson Block deliver a good presentation at a Value Investing Congress.

Block, if you don't know, is the founder of Muddy Waters Research. He's a short seller. And he is most famous for bringing down Sino-Forest in 2011.

Carson's report alleged Sino-Forest was a fraud and its shares were worthless—claims backed up by convincing research. Sino-Forest fell 89 percent after Block's report. Even a few famous superstar investors had got hung up on that one. John Paulson—the man who made over $1 billion personally after smoking out fraud in the subprime market in 2007—lost $700 million in Sino-Forest.

So, Block is a super sleuth. When his reports come out, the targeted company's share price crumbles. He keeps the bad guys up at night.

Well, Block thinks we live in an "age of venality." There is an unprecedented willingness to do dishonest things in return for money.

"Greed and short-term thinking are more prevalent than they've ever been," Block said. It's hard to prove that. But when markets are high, there is no question that's when the shysters like to come out and pick the pockets of complacent investors.

Block's presentation was all about the ways in which the system works against investors. Let's go through them.

On Management

"The first element that tilts the odd [sic] against investors is management," Block said. There are good and bad management teams, of course. But to generalize: Block said incentives are often short-term. They encourage risky betting.

And the CEOs themselves are largely charismatic. "That's how you get to lead an organization," Block said. "It's easy to fall for their charm."

He reminded us that Andrew Fastow, the CEO of Enron before it went under, won *CFO Magazine*'s "Award for Excellence in 1999." Enron, as you know, was a huge fraud.

Block says the more success and awards and public adulation a CEO earns, the less likely they are to own up to mistakes. Fastow himself has said as much. And Fastow quoted *Moby Dick*—"which he read while he was in prison"—to that effect. (See top quote.)

"Other people around the CEO can be expected to protect senior management," Block said. This makes deceptions harder to detect.

How can you deal with it?

Block had a good suggestion. "Management is better seen than heard." First, do your work, and only then, talk with management. "If I were to shake hands and like the people, I think that would really cloud my judgment." This is an important admission. Even Block says he can't resist the charms of management.

Here's his advice:

- Reading conference-call transcripts is better than listening to them.
- Read several quarters at a time to look for disappearing initiatives, changes in language.
- Are questions ever evaded? Which ones? "Sometimes they call on the same people and they have a rapport with them," Block said. You know; it's the calls that go like this: "Great quarter, guys." "Thanks, Mike." If the transcript is filled with that and there are no pointed questions, then it "smells like a stage-managed call."

In summary, it is "best to keep management at a distance."

On Boards

Boards are supposed to represent shareholders, but they don't. As Block said, there is a symbiotic relationship with CEOs. Board members often view their directorship as a perk, not a responsibility. Insurance and other protections insulate boards from liability.

Moreover, board investigations into misdeeds are unreliable. When boards have to investigate something, it's like asking them to admit their own incompetence, Block said. You can't rely on them.

Lawyers

Lawyers "make it difficult for investors to make good decisions." They represent the interests of their clients—the people who pay them—not investors.

"'Prestigious' law firms are a surprisingly effective fig leaf," Block said. They are great at writing indecipherable prose. And the attorney–client privilege "hides innumerable acts of corporate wrongdoing."

Which means, don't be fooled because a firm has a fancy lawyer.

Auditors

"Auditors are completely misunderstood," Block said. Again, they represent the interest of their clients—the people who pay them. I'm reminded of the old saying "Whose bread I eat, his song I sing."

Block talked about how it is a profession that rewards failure. Negative audits often lead to lifetime employment because the firm is fearful of being sued and wants the auditor around to help get it out of any messes.

Further, Block said, accounting is "a profession fighting against accountability and transparency. They [the big auditing firms] fight disclosures repeatedly. They do not want to provide investors with a better window into audits."

He also reminded us that audits are not "clean bills of health" and do not detect fraud. In fact, he said, in the Sino-Forest case, Ernst & Young (the auditor) was Sino-Forest's best friend. He shared a disclosure E&Y wrote: "The majority of the accounts receivable arising from sales of standing timber are realized through instructing the debtors to settle the amounts payable on standing timber and other liabilities denominated in Renminbi."

Can you make heads or tails of that?

Block translated it thusly: it means the company never collected the cash. Put another way, "95%+ of the company's reported gross profit in 16 years of being public never went into the company's bank accounts!!!"

Messy, indecipherable disclosures are clues to stay away.

Investment Banks

Obviously, the investment banks have an incentive to sell financial products—stocks, bonds, and so on. They are not looking out for your interest.

If you don't know this by now, here it is: don't look to research put out by investment banks or brokerage houses as a source of advice on where you should invest.

Market-Research Firms

This one was interesting because you often see "market research" quoted from the likes of Frost & Sullivan and iResearch. Block said companies hire these firms and often give them the research to get the report they want. Market research is there to add legitimacy to management's claims. It's not to help you make a good decision.

Distrust market research. Look for more objective sources of information, such as actual sales data and trends.

China

Taking China as a category unto itself, Block had a good line: "China is to stock fraud what Silicon Valley is to technology."

He believes investors are getting complacent again about fraud risks in China. And he points out, "no fraudster from China has ever been meaningfully punished for defrauding North American investors."

Phelps said in his book an investor going overseas was often simply swapping risks he could see for risks he couldn't see. Investing is hard. Investing overseas, in a foreign market, is harder.

Precautions to Take

There is always a risk you'll get snookered somewhere. Most investors who have been in the game long enough have been fooled at some point—even if only in smaller ways than in a Sino-Forest-type event.

But it's important to make a distinction here. There is bias, and then there is lying. There is salesmanship, and then there is fraud. Almost all management teams aim to put a positive gloss on what they are doing. But we know that, and that's not fraud.

There are some things you can do to avoid the big frauds and scam artists.

I say the best thing to do is invest with management teams that own a lot of stock. That is often a great bulwark against fraud in the United States. But that by itself is not enough, since many China frauds, for instance, had big insider ownership.

Second, partner up with people who have had success. If you stick with people with a track record of success, it is unlikely you will step into a fraud like Sino-Forest.

Third, stay away from weird things—you know, companies that do things you can't understand. If you don't understand how they make money—see Sino-Forest—run!

Fourth, avoid the hot sectors of whatever market you're in. Biotech has been hot. No surprise that a number of short ideas presented at the congress were biotech. That's where promoters and shysters go because that's where they can get the biggest bang for the buck. The sector is rife with fraud.

Ditto anything engaged in "social media" or "cloud computing" or any of the other buzzwords making the rounds. Be careful around companies that seem to be created mainly to scratch an investor's itch.

Remember, a few years ago, people wanted ways to invest in a housing recovery. Then boom, all these housing REITs start popping up. Be careful. They may not be frauds, but they are probably not great investments.

When it comes to fraud, I always think of a line from Phelps, who dedicated a chapter to stock manipulation: "In Africa, where there are no antelope, there are no lions."

By taking some reasonable steps, you can avoid becoming prey.

Do Ignore Forecasters

Investing is tough for a lot of people because they expect they can trust the opinion of experts. Yet in the world of markets, the so-called experts get an awful lot wrong. However, if you look carefully at the kinds of errors they make, you can weave a reliable investment approach from the cloth of human folly.

For example, look at earnings estimates. Wall Street analysts publish earnings estimates for stocks. Investors often aggregate these estimates to come up with a "consensus." When earnings come out, the media will talk about how such and such a company beat or missed the consensus. A good beating can send a stock up strongly, while a miss can send it tumbling.

Many investors watch these estimates like hawks and rely on them in their buy and sell decisions. The problem is these estimates are wrong often, and by a wide margin. One large study covered nearly 95,000 consensus estimates from more than two decades. It found the average estimate was off by more than 40 percent!

David Dreman writes about this in his book *Contrarian Investment Strategies*. Digging deeper, he finds the analysts made consistent errors in one direction: they were too optimistic.

So if you put the two together, you quickly come to realize the odds of you owning a stock that doesn't suffer a negative earnings surprise is pretty small. In fact, the odds of a single stock getting through four quarters without a negative surprise of at least 10 percent worse than expected are only one in four.

I don't mean to pick on analysts only. As a species, we are by nature optimistic—at least most of us are. It's the winning trait in the evolutionary derby, and we need to invest taking into account that optimism.

To illustrate his findings, Dreman included a great chart that showed consensus forecasts for interest rates over a period of time. One big thing sticks out. People tended to forecast a future that closely approximated the present. Reality was much more volatile. Forecasters face many surprises.

So, it is important to knock down the pedestals on which forecasters sit.

Jason Zweig and Rodney Sullivan recently published a collection of Benjamin Graham's essays and speeches in *Benjamin Graham: Building a Profession*. Graham is widely cited as the dean of security analysis. And the title of this book is inspired by a witty line by Adam Smith (pseudonym for commentator George Goodman). Smith wrote, "The reason that Graham is the undisputed dean is that before him there was no profession and after him they began to call it that."

As I read over these essays—some of which I remember having read in other places—one theme stuck out that is good to keep in mind today. Speaking of the financial community generally—the gamut of analysts, economists, investors and the like—Graham laid out this criticism: "They tend to take the market and themselves too seriously. They spend a large part of their time trying, valiantly and ineffectively, to do things they can't do well."

What sorts of things? Among them is "to forecast short- or long-term changes in the economy, and in the price level of common stocks."

Many people spend a great deal of time trying to guess where the economy or the stock market is going. And yet, there are countless studies that show the folly of such forecasting.

James Montier of GMO, a global money management firm, highlighted how poor economists are at forecasting. He concludes,

> Attempting to invest on the back of economic forecasts is an exercise in extreme folly, even in normal times. Economists are probably the one group who make astrologers look like professionals when it comes to telling the future. . . . They have missed every recession in the last four decades! And it isn't just growth that economists can't forecast: it's also inflation, bond yields, and pretty much everything else.

He shares a chart that captures the consensus GDP forecast and how GDP really fared. It's interesting to see because one conclusion immediately jumps out at you. Take a look at the chart below and see whether you agree.

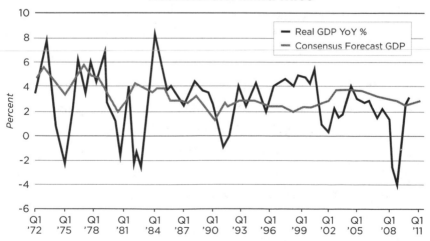

Economists: blind mice

Note how the consensus never gets the extremes. The consensus always forecasts a middle ground. The same general pattern of error holds
for all kinds of forecasting, including forecasted earnings per share and
market prices. The problem is, of course, that the extremes are where you
make (or lose) a lot of money. Consensus forecasts aren't worth much,
whether right or not.

	Consensus Forecast	Nonconsensus Forecast
Accurate	Average	Above Average
Not Accurate	Average	Below Average

Finally, Howard Marks at Oaktree Capital once put together the following schematic, which makes things clear. It shows you the return you
get from each type of forecast, based on whether it is accurate or not.

"Extraordinary performance comes only from correct non-consensus
forecasts," Marks writes. He uses the example of interest rates in 1978,
which then stood at 8 percent. Most people thought they'd stay there. Bulls
said they'd go to 9 percent; bears said they'd go to 7 percent. Marks says,
"Most of the time rates would have been in that range and no one would
have made much money. The big profits went to those who predicted 15%
long bond yields. But where were those people? Extreme predictions are
rarely right, but they're the ones that make you the big money."

Ben Graham's greatest student was Warren Buffett—also a great ig-
norer of forecasts. In his 1994 shareholder letter, Buffett showed he had
taken Graham's lesson to heart:

> We will continue to ignore political and economic forecasts which
> are an expensive distraction for many investors and businessmen.
> Thirty years ago, no one could have foreseen the huge expansion of
> the Vietnam War, wage and price controls, two oil shocks, the resigna-
> tion of a president, the dissolution of the Soviet Union, a one-day drop
> in the Dow of 508 points, or treasury bill yields fluctuating between
> 2.8% and 17.4%. . . . But, surprise—none of these blockbuster events
> made the slightest dent in Ben Graham's investment principles.

I often hear sweeping pronouncements made about the stock market and where it's going from pundits and investors everywhere, as I'm sure you do too. I also notice how so many people take such guesses seriously. However, I'm not going to suggest we should all stop guessing. That's asking too much.

But I'd advise holding all such opinions loosely and with a great deal of humility. After all, how many people in March 2009 thought the market would rally 80 percent in less than two years? Not many, that's for sure. Yet, it happened. No one could have forecast the Gulf oil spill happening when it did, either.

Over the course of an investing life, stuff is going to happen—both good and bad—that no one saw coming. Instead of playing the guessing game, focus on the opportunities in front of you.

And there are always, in all markets, many opportunities. Yes, always!

Graham pointed out—in 1976—there were over 5,000 publicly traded securities. (Today there are over three times that number, especially if you consider the international markets.) Then he said, "Following a wide variety of approaches and preferences, the individual investor should at all times be able to locate at least 1% of the total list—say, thirty issues or more—that offer attractive buying opportunities."

That's true. When someone tells me they can't find anything worth buying in this market, they are just not looking hard enough. With 10,000 securities today, even one-half of 1 percent is 50 names. Kind of makes you think, doesn't it?

What I've Learned from Over a Decade of Writing Newsletters

I started writing newsletters professionally in February 2004. Before that, I was a freelance writer, investment hobbyist and professional banker (corporate lender, to be exact). After I hit the 10-year mark, I thought it was a good time to look back over the results. So, I finally got my letter's track record independently verified.

The results showed a 28 percent average return, or 16 percent annualized. Given these exceptional results, what can I say about how they came about? Well, I will share a few quirkier aspects of investing I've learned the hard way—things you might not think about.

Sosnoff's law. This comes from a book called *Humble on Wall Street*, published in 1975 and still one of the best books on the experience of investing, on what it feels like. Its author, Martin Sosnoff, wrote that "the price of a stock varies inversely with the thickness of its research file. The fattest files are found in stocks that are the most troublesome and will decline the furthest. The thinnest files are reserved for those that appreciate the most."

In other words, the best ideas are often the simplest. If I find myself working really hard to justify keeping or buying a stock, I think of Sosnoff's law. I've wasted countless hours on bad stocks and bad businesses.

Many great investors have some version of this truism. (Peter Lynch comes to mind: "Never invest in any idea you can't illustrate with a crayon.") Simplicity is best.

Beware of "fixed ideas." Max Stirner was a German philosopher who wrote a bombshell of a book published in 1845. English speakers know it as *The Ego and His Own*. It is a difficult book but full of powerful concepts. Stirner contended that people do not have ideas. Rather, their ideas have them. These "fixed ideas" then rule over their thinking.

Stirner wrote that a thought was your own only when you "have no misgiving about bringing it in danger of death at every moment." He actually looked forward to having his own ideas tested and knocked down: "I shall look forward smilingly to the outcome of the battle, smilingly lay the shield on the corpses of my thoughts and my faith, smilingly triumph when I am beaten. That is the very humor of the thing."

In markets, you see many people with fixed ideas. They are the ones who always recommend gold, no matter what. They are the ones always expecting the market to crash, forever obsessed with the Fed or the theories of dead economists. They are the ones always expecting the dollar to crash. They are the ones who can't change their mind.

I have learned, painfully, to think like Stirner. I have no attachment to ideas. I have no problem changing my mind. In fact, I look forward to doing so and actively try to poke holes in my own ideas and theories.

Be suspicious of abstractions. Here I borrow from another favorite sage, that corncob-pipe-smoking disheveled man of letters Paul Goodman. "I can't think abstractly," he wrote. "I start from concrete experience." He cracked that because he stuck so close to concrete experience, he "cannot really write fiction."

People take easily, though, to big ideas: The new economy. Peak oil. The Chinese century. The Great Moderation. All of these things are just abstract ideas. They are predictions about how the world might look. But they are far from concrete experience—and hence likely to lead you astray. And each of the abstractions I mentioned has led investors astray.

"Investment," author John Train once wrote, "is the craft of the specific." It's about why A is a better investment than B. "It's extraordinary how much time the public spends on the unknowable." I've learned to identify and accept the unknowable. I've learned to distrust grand theories.

Investing is a people business. Early on, I relied on reported numbers and I screened for statistical cheapness. I'd look for low P/E stocks, for example. Everyone can see these numbers. Yet, these methods can still work well. Over time, however, I've learned that knowing what the numbers don't show is worth more than any statistic.

I like ideas where the story is not obvious from the numbers alone. I want to find that something else is going on in the business that makes it attractive. These are rare, but the rewards of investing with them are often great. Howard Hughes is a perfect example. Spun out of General Growth Properties in 2010, it screened terribly. No earnings. No dividend. But it was in a great situation that required some understanding of the potential of its development projects. And it delivered extraordinary returns, up fourfold in just a few years.

To find a situation like this requires a lot of reading and networking. I talk to a lot of people in the course of a year—investors, executives, analysts and economists. Ideas can come from anywhere. But my best ideas often come from people. Hidden stories exist. And there is a person, somewhere, who knows that story.

Make an effort to find those people and their stories.

100-Bagger Miscellany

Here's more miscellany on 100-baggers and how to get them.

Investing abroad. Investing abroad is a way to expand the menu. However, if you are investing abroad to flee risks at home, I'd check that impulse. I know some Americans are interested in investing abroad because they are so down on US politics or the US economy or whatever.

Phelps made a good point in his book that I will repeat here. He said when we invest abroad we often trade risks we see for risks we can't see or are not aware of. Be mindful of this. Many investors have had their heads handed to them in far-off lands that seemed alluring. It's happened to me more than once.

Having said that, the principles in this book are universal and timeless and apply to all markets everywhere.

Inflation. Throughout this book, I've dealt in nominal dollars, unadjusted for inflation. This doesn't mean inflation isn't real, of course. Odds are, if you stick US dollars under a mattress for 10 years, you're going to lose purchasing power. Put another way, $20 may get you a haircut today, but it probably won't in 10 years.

My main message to you is to not obsess over it. Again, I speak from experience. I know many who get so hung up on worrying about the US dollar that they confine themselves to investing in gold stocks and natural-resource companies as they worry about the end of the world.

This is extremely costly. The best inflation fighters are 100-baggers. They are so good at beating inflation that I can talk about inflation in a few paragraphs.

I've taken to reading Warren Buffett's annual letters—50 of them—from first to last, something I've never done. What's interesting about the early letters is the amount of time given to discussing inflation and its effects on investors.

Inflation has not been a serious problem for years now. But investors tend to prepare for yesterday's battles, which Buffett acknowledges. "While investors and managers must place their feet in the future, their memories and nervous systems often remain plugged into the past," Buffett wrote in 1981.

This reminds me of Peter Lynch's example from Mayan mythology. A great flood destroyed the world. So, the Mayans moved to higher ground in the woods. Then fire destroyed the world. So they moved away from the woods and built houses of stone. Then came an earthquake. . . .

Inflation was high in the late 1970s and was a real problem for businesses and investors. It was something new, and people were slow to take in what it meant.

What it meant was that a 20 percent return was not really a 20 percent return, but could actually be negative after inflation and taxes—the "investor's misery index," as Buffett called it.

Buffett gave an analogy:

If you (a) forego ten hamburgers to purchase an investment; (b) receive dividends which, after tax, buy two hamburgers; and (c) receive, upon sale of your holdings, after-tax proceeds that will buy eight hamburgers, then (d) you have had no real income from your investment, no matter how much it appreciated in dollars. You may feel richer, but you won't eat richer.

He does not mince words about what those high inflation rates did to the returns of Berkshire. In the 1981 letter, he wrote about how inflation made Berkshire's "apparently satisfactory results . . . illusory as a measure of true investment results for our owners."

In the 1979 letter he wrote this:

One friendly but sharp-eyed commentator on Berkshire has pointed out that our book value at the end of 1964 would have bought about one-half ounce of gold and, fifteen years later, after we have plowed back all earnings along with much blood, sweat and tears, the book value produced will buy about the same half ounce.

A similar comparison could be drawn with Middle Eastern oil. The rub has been that government has been exceptionally able in printing money and creating promises, but is unable to print gold or create oil.

Keeping up with inflation was a triumph. Most American businesses chewed up capital and left owners with less purchasing power than they started with.

In 1981, Buffett pointed out that tax-exempt bonds paid 14 percent. And that 14 percent went right into the investor's pocket. American business also earned 14 percent that year. But that did not go directly into the investor's pocket. Even if a business earning 14 percent paid out all of its earnings in dividends, taxes would reduce your return below inflation.

How can you value such a business in such an environment?

Buffett uses the analogy of a bond. Let's say you had a tax-exempt bond issued in prior years that paid you 7 percent. Such a bond would be worth 50 percent of its par value in an environment where tax-exempt bonds pay 14 percent.

And so it is with stocks.

"Thus," Buffett wrote, "*with interest rates on passive investments at late 1981 levels*, a typical American business is no longer worth one hundred cents on the dollar to owners who are individuals." (italics in the original)

The year 1982 was the last year of that kind of inflation, which diminished thereafter. No wonder it proved to be such a great bottom in the stock market. As rates fell, businesses became more and more valuable.

This explains why interest rates are a big deal and why people are so keen on what the Fed is going to do. Interest rates on passive, tax-exempt securities set the crossbar for stocks.

Here's Buffett summing it up well:

Inflationary experience and expectations will be major (but not the only) factors affecting the height of the crossbar in future years. If the causes of long-term inflation can be tempered, passive returns are likely to fall and the intrinsic position of American equity capital should significantly improve. Many businesses that now must be classified as economically "bad" would be restored to the "good" category under such circumstances.

Inflation did abate. Rates fell. Stocks soared.

While on the topic of Buffett and inflation, it's worth clearing up another misconception about what kinds of businesses do better in inflationary environments.

As much as the big-picture crowd likes to hammer away at stocks, they do have a soft spot for stocks with tangible assets—such as gold miners and oil stocks. The usual belief is these stocks will protect you when the dollar loses value.

Not really true.

I always think about Warren Buffett's example from his 1983 letter, when inflation was still high on everyone's list of concerns. Buffett ran through an example of See's Candies versus a hypothetical business with lots of tangible assets—let's call the latter Gold-Oil Co.

Both businesses earn $2 million in profits. See's has little in the way of tangible assets—about $4 million worth. The stock goes for $25 million. Gold-Oil Co, by contrast, has $18 million in net tangible assets supporting its operations. Since it earns a lower return on its asset base, the stock goes for $18 million (basically the value of its net tangible assets).

Now, let's roll forward and say inflation doubles prices. Both need to double their earnings just to keep pace with inflation. As Buffett writes, "this would seem to be no great trick: just sell the same number of units at double earlier prices and, assuming profit margins remain unchanged, profits also must double."

But here's the kicker: both businesses will need to double their investment in tangible assets, too. As Buffett writes,

Both businesses probably would have to double their nominal investment in net tangible assets, since that is the kind of economic requirement that inflation usually imposes on businesses, both good and bad . . . and all of this inflation-required investment will produce no improvement in rate of return. The motivation for this investment is the survival of the business, not the prosperity of the owner.

For See's, this means $8 million in additional investment. For Gold-Oil Co., this means $18 million in additional investment.

Buffett paid $25 million to own See's. After this round of inflation, See's "might be worth $50 million if valued (as it logically would be) on the same basis is [sic] was at the time of our purchase."

Thus, See's would have gained $25 million in nominal value on $8 million of additional investment. That's more than three to one. As for Gold-Oil Co., it might be still be worth the value of its net tangible assets, now $36 million. That's an $18 million rise in value on $18 million of additional investment. That's 1 to 1.

Note that inflation was bad for both. But it was less bad for See's, which owned little in tangible assets. This idea has been hard for many people to grasp, as Buffett notes:

> For years the traditional wisdom—long on tradition, short on wisdom—held that inflation protection was best provided by businesses laden with natural resources, plants and machinery, or other tangible assets ("In Goods We Trust"). It doesn't work that way. Asset-heavy businesses generally earn low rates of return—rates that often barely provide enough capital to fund the inflationary needs of the existing business, with nothing left over for real growth, for distribution to owners, or for acquisition of new businesses.

This idea is critical. If you don't understand this, you should read through the example again. Work it out on paper for yourself. Change the numbers around if you wish. It's important to understand the dynamics. In a world of monetary depreciation, the asset-light company wins. Or put another way, monetary depreciation favors the asset light.

The irony for the big-picture crowd is though they tend to shun stocks, when they do get involved they favor the worst kinds.

To quote another great investor, John Maynard Keynes: "The difficulty lies not in the new ideas but in escaping from the old ones." The ideal business during an inflationary time is one that can (a) raise prices easily and (b) doesn't require investment in a lot of assets.

What about the Failures, the Stocks That Didn't Make It?

This is a question that comes up. People wonder about the companies that looked like 100-baggers but didn't make it for whatever reason. I mentioned this earlier when discussing the limitations of this study.

First, I'd say there can be no failures. If you compound capital at 20 percent annually, you will multiply that capital a hundredfold after 25 years. There is no failure in the same way as if I were testing, say, stocks with ROEs above 20 percent.

Second, I don't know how I would go about studying failures. How would you define failure? When you think it through, it's not so easy. So, instead, I took the path that Phelps took. I decided to focus on the 100-baggers.

I humbly offer up this study as a way to increase our understanding of these magical stocks. Nothing is perfect, including this study. I can only hope others will share their own experiences and studies and improve our understanding even more in the future.

CHAPTER 14:

IN CASE OF THE NEXT GREAT DEPRESSION

The title of this chapter is a bit tongue-in-cheek, but it's worth spending some time talking about what happens if (when) we get a really bad outcome in the stock market—such as a 2008-style crash.

I addressed this question in chapter 3, but I'll expand on the discussion here. (See the subsection "A Coffee Can for the Apocalypse.") In essence, hunting for 100-baggers is completely independent of whatever is happening in the market. You should never stop looking for 100-baggers, bear market or bull.

But since you will likely quit only when the market turns ugly, that's what I'll focus on.

Phelps says as much, and I already quoted his comment about how "bear market smoke gets in one's eyes" and prevents you from keeping up the search. It should be obvious that if you'd bought Apple 15 years ago, you really needn't have cared what the Fed was doing or what the latest readings were on the economy or any of the worthless stuff investors pay attention to.

And no matter how bad things seem to get, there is always opportunity.

There is no better way to see that, at least anecdotally, than by looking back at the Great Depression. This was the greatest economic calamity the United States ever had to suffer through. And yet, if you really dig into the era, you will find stories of people who did well even in this most difficult period.

My goal is not to say the Great Depression wasn't difficult. It's not to offer up some new interpretation of what happened or to paint it in a better light. It was a disaster. The point is that people planted seeds for great fortunes then. It may seem obvious that lower prices, as found in such disasters, create "easier" opportunities to make hundredfold returns.

But bad times discourage people from investing. I've seen it happen. In 2008, when the stock market tanked, many people I know were afraid to invest.

Pull this chapter out when the market crashes.

Marty Whitman: On Market Comebacks

Marty Whitman, who managed the Third Avenue Value Fund, wrote a letter to his shareholders about "market comebacks" as the whole 2007–2008 crisis unfolded. In that letter are some wise ideas.

First, Whitman makes a general comment that seems reasonable enough: "General markets tend to come back strongly in periods subsequent to price crashes! That was the case in 1932, 1937, 1962, 1974–75, 1980–82, 1987 and 2001–2002. A comeback also seems likely after the unprecedented crash of 2007–2008."

Okay, so far, we can all agree. But here's the hitch for investors in stocks. Not all stocks are likely to come back. This is where the letter gets interesting. Whitman identifies three types of stock unlikely to participate to any extent in any price comeback.

The first category includes stocks that were grossly overpriced to begin with. If you paid stupid prices for your stocks, this is where that mistake will cause you pain. Otherwise, price declines should by themselves deter you from keeping a stock. Whitman makes the point that many of his stocks increased in net asset value (NAV) despite the fact that most of these stocks "declined by 30% to 70% in 2008." Whitman believed many of his stocks could triple or quadruple and still trade cheap relative to NAV. If you have a legit 100-bagger candidate, the same could easily be true.

The second type of stock unlikely to recover is one that suffers a "permanent impairment." The ultimate permanent impairment is when a firm goes out of business. But it could also be a significant loss. Basically, the idea here is that something has changed and the business is no longer capable of doing what it once was.

The third and final category includes stocks "subject to massive dilution during the meltdown where old common stockholders were unable to protect themselves from the dilution." This happens when a company issues a bunch of new shares to raise money to cover losses or pay back debt. It's like adding water to your beer and sharing it.

A famous economist learned these lessons the hard way.

A Famous Economist Learns to Buy Right and Hold On

"A falling stock market seems to clarify and stimulate thought. When it is rising, nobody cares to know why or how, but when it falls everyone is very eager to know all about it."

— Albert Jay Nock, *Informed Common Sense: The Journals of Albert Jay Nock*

Take the following, type it out and pin it over your desk:

I feel no shame at being found still owning a share when the bottom of the market comes. I do not think it is the business, far less the duty, of an institutional or any other serious investor to be constantly considering whether he should cut and run on a falling market, or to feel himself open to blame if shares depreciate in his hands. I would go much further than that. I should say it is from time to time the duty of a serious investor to accept the depreciation of his holdings with equanimity and without reproaching himself.

That excerpt comes from a letter in 1938 by one of the greatest investors of all time. He made money in one of the most difficult markets of all time—that of the Great Depression.

He is John Maynard Keynes (1883–1946).

This may surprise you. Keynes you know as an influential economist. But whatever you think of Keynes as an economist, the man was a great investor. He had a keen understanding of markets.

Keynes managed Cambridge's King's College Chest Fund. The fund averaged 12 percent per year from 1927–1946, which was remarkable given that the period seemed to be all about gray skies and storm clouds—it included the Great Depression and World War II. The UK stock market fell 15 percent during this stretch. And to top it off, the Chest Fund's returns included only capital appreciation, as the college spent the income earned in the portfolio, which was considerable. I think it must be one of the most remarkable track records in the annals of finance.

How he did it is the subject of this section.

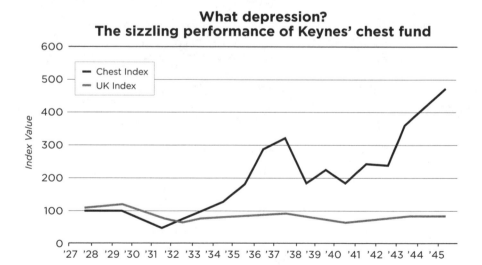

Keynes also made himself a personal fortune as an investor. When he died, he left an estate worth some $30 million in present-day dollars, which surprised his contemporaries. Justyn Walsh, author of *Keynes and the Market*, points out that Keynes spent his last six years as an unpaid

Treasury adviser. He outlived his parents, who left him no inheritance. And Keynes was a great patron of the arts, financing many ventures out of his own pocket. To finish with such a grand sum sent London society abuzz.

"Some surprise has been expressed about the large fortune left by Lord Keynes," reflected the *Financial Times*. "Yet Lord Keynes was one of the few economists with the practical ability to make money."

Keynes began as a run-of-mill speculator and trader, trying to anticipate trends and forecast cycles. The Great Crash of 1929 sent him back to the drawing board.

Keynes was, in fact, nearly wiped out in the Great Crash. His personal net worth fell by more than 80 percent. He then had a great conversion. Trading the market demanded "abnormal foresight" and "phenomenal skill" to work, he concluded. "I am clear," the new Keynes wrote in a memorandum, "that the idea of wholesale shifts [in and out of the market at different stages of the business cycle] is for various reasons impracticable and undesirable."

After the crash, he became an investor, rather than a speculator. His new ideas on investing began to presage those of value-investing icons Ben Graham and Warren Buffett. Interestingly, the crash hurt Graham too and motivated him also to think deeply about the process of investing. The two great money minds came to nearly the same place in their thinking.

Keynes now focused less on forecasting the market. Instead, he cast his keen mind on individual securities, trying to figure out their "ultimate values," as he called them. He summed up his new philosophy in a note to a colleague: "My purpose is to buy securities where I am satisfied as to assets and ultimate earnings power and where the market price seems cheap in relation to these."

He also became more patient. Giving an example, Keynes described how it was easier and safer in the long run to buy a 75-cent dollar and wait, rather than buy a 75-cent dollar and sell it because it became a 50-cent dollar—and hope to buy it back as a 40-cent dollar. Keynes learned to trust more in his own research and opinions and not let market prices put him off a good deal. When the market fell, Keynes remarked, "I do not draw from this conclusion that a responsible investing body should every week cast panic glances over its list of securities to find one more victim to fling to the bears."

Keynes also developed a fierce contrarian streak. One of his greatest personal coups came in 1933. The Great Depression was on. Franklin Delano Roosevelt's speeches gushed with anticorporate rhetoric. The market sank. America's utilities were, Keynes noticed, extremely cheap in "what is for the time being an irrationally unfashionable market." He bought the depressed preferred stocks. In the next year, his personal net worth would nearly triple.

Keynes was an adviser to an insurance company, as well as manager of the Chest Fund. In a note, Keynes laid out his understanding of the quirky, contrarian nature of investing. It is "the one sphere of life and activity where victory, security and success is always to the minority, and never to the majority. When you find anyone agreeing with you, change your mind. When I can persuade the board of my insurance company to buy a share, that, I am learning from experience, is the right moment for selling it."

He also learned to hold onto his stocks "through thick and thin," he said, to let the magic of compounding do its thing (in a tax-free fashion too, by avoiding capital gains taxes). "'Be quiet'" is our best motto," he wrote, by which he meant to ignore the short-term noise and let the longer-term forces assert themselves. It also meant limiting his activities to buying only when he found intrinsic values far above stock prices.

Keynes also came to the conclusion that you could own too many stocks. Better to own fewer stocks and more of your very best ideas than spread yourself too thin. Committees and others repeatedly criticized Keynes for making big bets on a smaller number of companies. In a typically witty reply, Keynes defended his views. In this case, his critics accused him of making too large a bet on Elder Dempster: "Sorry to have gone too large on Elder Dempster. I was suffering from my chronic delusion that one good share is safer than 10 bad ones."

He rejected the idea, as Buffett and other great investors have, that you should dilute your best bets by holding a long list of stocks. At times during Keynes's career, half of his portfolio might be in only a handful of names, though he liked to mix up the risks he took. So though five names might make up half of his portfolio, they wouldn't be all gold stocks, for instance. "For his faith in portfolio concentration," Walsh writes, "Keynes was rewarded with an investment performance far superior—albeit more volatile—than that of the broader market."

In the depth of the Depression, Keynes lost a friend, Sidney Russell Cooke, who took his own life after suffering severe losses in the market. Keynes, perhaps reflecting on this experience, wrote that investors need to take losses with "as much equanimity and patience" as possible. Investors must accept that stock prices can swing wide of underlying values for extended stretches of time.

Keynes's investment performance improved markedly after adopting these ideas. Whereas in the 1920s he generally trailed the market, he was a great performer after the crash. Walsh dates Keynes's adoption of what we might think of as a Warren Buffett sort of approach as beginning in 1931. From that time to 1945, the Chest Fund rose tenfold in value in 15 years, versus no return for the overall market. That is a truly awesome performance in an awfully tough environment.

Keynes, perhaps poring over stock tables

A more recent paper is "Keynes the Stock Market Investor," by David Chambers and Elroy Dimson. They add more interesting details about how his investing style changed. As Chambers and Dimson note, "As a young man, Keynes was supremely self-assured about his capabilities, and he traded most actively to the detriment of performance in the first period of his stewardship of the College endowment up to the early 1930s."

In the early 1930s, he changed his approach. With the exception of 1938, he would never trail the market again. This change showed up in a number of ways. First, he traded less frequently. He became more patient and more focused on the long-term.

Here is his portfolio turnover by decade:

1921–1929	55%
1930–1939	30%
1940–1946	14%

Turnover was just one aspect of Keynes's change. Another was how he reacted during market declines. From 1929 to 1930, Keynes sold one-fifth of his holdings and switched to bonds. But when the market fell in the 1937–1938, he added to his positions. He stayed 90 percent invested throughout.

This is a remarkable change. It again reflects less concern about short-term stock prices. He was clearly more focused on the value of what he owned, as his letters show. The authors of the paper note of Keynes's change, "Essentially, he switched from a macro market-timing approach to bottom-up stock-picking."

In a memorandum in May of 1938, Keynes offered the best summing up of his own philosophy:

1. careful selection of a few investments (or a few types of investment) based on their cheapness in relation to their probable actual and potential intrinsic value over a period of years ahead and in relation to alternative investments;

2. a steadfast holding of these investments in fairly large units through thick and thin, perhaps for several years, until either they have fulfilled their promise or it has become evident that their purchase was a mistake; and

3. a balanced investment position, that is, a portfolio exposed to a variety of risks in spite of individual holdings being large, and if possible, opposed risks.

Here is one last bit of advice from the same memo:

In the main, therefore, slumps are experiences to be lived through and survived with as much equanimity and patience as possible. Advantage can be taken of them more because individual securities fall out of their reasonable parity with other securities on such occasions, than by attempts at wholesale shifts into and out of equities as a whole. One must not allow one's attitude to securities which have a daily market quotation to be disturbed by this fact.

If these ideas were good enough for the Great Depression, they're good enough for whatever comes next now.

Floyd Odlum: Making the Best of Bad Times

Floyd Odlum is sometimes described as the only guy to make a fortune in the Great Depression. (He wasn't.)

James Grant, editor of *Grant's Interest Rate Observer*, called Odlum a "salvage artist par excellence." "None of us can know the future," Grant wrote. "But, like Odlum, we can make the best of a sometimes unappetizing present."

Grant also managed to scrounge up a pretty good anecdote on Odlum. In the summer of 1933, when all the world seemed to be in pieces, Odlum strolled into his office, looked at his glum partners and said, "I believe there's a better chance to make money now than ever before."

Odlum liked poking around in the smoking wreckage of the 1930s. Bad times create wonderful pricing. The story of a man with the odd name of Odlum is one of how he got rich in the Great Depression.

Floyd Bostwick Odlum was a lawyer and industrialist, born in 1892. He started his investing career in 1923 with $39,000. In a couple of years, he turned that into $700,000 through some savvy investing in deeply undervalued stocks and other securities. Odlum was on his way. All told, in about 15 years he parlayed that $39,000 into over $100 million.

His big score came after the crash of 1929. Odlum bought busted-up investment trusts. As Diana Henriques writes in *The White Sharks of Wall Street*, "Odlum [became] a multimillionaire almost overnight by investing in the undervalued shares of twenty-two investment trusts decimated by the 1929 crash."

He found companies trading for less than the value of the cash and securities they owned. So he bought them, liquidated them and then took the cash and did it again . . . and again. Of course, to do this, he had to have a little money at the bottom. And he did.

Odlum was either lucky or prescient, because he avoided much of the pain of the 1929 crash by selling some of his investments beforehand— leaving him with some $14 million of fresh cash to take advantage of opportunities. So, don't be afraid to hold onto cash until you find those special 100-bagger opportunities.

As Odlum's career shows, bad times create those big opportunities.

Memories of the Great Depression— From A Wall Street Trader

Wall Street trader David Feldman lived through the Great Depression. In 1997, at the age of 87, he set down his thoughts in a little memoir titled *Ups and Downs of a Wall Street Trader during the Depth of the Great Depression of the 1930s*. It's interesting that he felt the need to append "of the 1930s" to his title, so as not to confuse it with others that would follow.

It was a brutal time. A short table of some issues selected at random by Feldman shows the damage:

Stock	1929 High	1932 Low
General Electric	403	8 1/2
Otis Elevator	450	9
Republic Steel	146 1/4	1 7/8
Warner Bros. Pictures	64 1/2	1/2
Johns-Manville	242 3/4	10
Spiegel-May-Stern	117 7/8	5/8

Another writer on the Depression, Frederick Lewis Allen, wrote about how the market was "so honeycombed with credit . . . [that it] became a beautifully contrived system for wrecking the price structure."

We saw that happen in 2008 with the forced liquidation of hedge funds and other investors operating with too much debt. Stocks dropped like birds shot out of the sky. Were the price drops entirely rational in every case? No.

And was General Electric really worth only $8.50 a share in 1932? How about Warner Brothers at 50 cents? No.

After the crash, people and businesses did cut back. There was also consolidation among businesses. In the 1930s, Allen notes, there was "more zeal for consolidating businesses than for expanding them or initiating them." With stock prices low, the cash-rich investors in corporate America had a chance to steal some things. Why invest in new oil wells when you can buy them on the stock market for less than half of what it would cost you to drill new ones? Why build new factories when you can buy a competitor for 20 cents on the dollar?

The aftermath of the crash is a good time to buy—with an important caveat, as Feldman points out: "Stock prices were *so low that so long as a company did not go out of business*, practically anything you might buy was certain to go up, if not sooner, then later." (italics added)

We might call this "Feldman's law of depression investing."

You can't be sure the stock you own won't fall from $16 to $1.50. In fact, I owned some stocks that did just that. But my stocks came back. Why? Because I was careful about owning stocks in good financial shape and with manageable debt levels. In cases where they did not come back and I was saddled with a big loss, it was always because I had invested in a weak balance sheet that couldn't hold up in the crisis.

Feldman's law is not as easy to apply as it may sound. By the end of 1933, more than 5,000 banks failed. Thousands of businesses also failed. Auburn Automobile, for instance, traded as high as $514 per share in 1929 and went to near 0 in 1933. I'm sure to investors in 1929, Auburn at zero in three years was unthinkable. Such is the way of financial disasters.

The economic devastation during the 1930s is hard to fathom. Statistics alone fail to capture it all, but what we have is breathtaking. The amount of money paid out in salaries dropped 40 percent from 1929 to 1932, according to the National Bureau of Economic Research. Dividends fell 56 percent. The unemployment rate was about 25 percent in 1932. In Buffalo, unemployment was 31 percent, which was not unusual among America's industrial cities.

A job in a South Carolina cotton mill might pay $8.25 per week for 11-hour shifts, five days a week. You were among the lucky if you got such a job. Children under 16 years of age toiled at textile mills for $3.10 per week.

Of course, a dollar was worth a lot more then than now. You could mail a letter for 2 cents and grab a cup of coffee for a nickel. The cost of gasoline was only 8 cents a gallon. Lunch might cost you a dollar. There were no lines.

An ounce of gold, before Roosevelt took the United States off the gold standard, was only $20.67. The exact same ounce of gold today would set you back about $1,400. "Some people have the rather naïve idea that a 2½% annual inflation rate is benign," writes David Feldman. "Actually, 2½ % is horrendous! Compounded over a period of ten years, it results in a 28% cost-of-living increase." (In terms of real returns, the 15 years following 1966 were worse for stock market investors than the 1930s because price inflation was so high. In the 1930s, prices fell.)

What did it all teach Feldman? He lost a lot of money in the crash and its aftermath, like almost everyone else. "One thing that this experience taught me was that, in investing, you should never cry over spilt milk," he writes. "Only the future is of importance."

In 2008, I didn't know whether we were headed for a 1930s-style depression. I think we were as close to such a precipice as at any time since the 1930s. As an investor, though, I knew—and wrote at the time—that valuations made it too compelling to leave the market then.

I also learned it was critically important to have some cash. "Cash was king," Feldman writes of the depths of the Great Depression. "If you happened to have any, you were really in the driver's seat." Cash means you have options and you are not reliant on fickle lenders.

As the 17th-century wanderer and memoirist Jack Casanova wrote, "My ill fortune no less than my good proved to me that . . . good comes from evil as evil comes from good." Likewise, 2008 was a good fortune in disguise that allowed investors to pick up new holdings on the cheap.

So again we see the wisdom of the lessons learned from Odlum: it's good to have cash and not be afraid to buy when things look bad.

John Dix: Avoid Debt

After the crash of 1929, the market had a nice recovery. By April of 1930, the market was up 41 percent from its low on November 13, 1929. Many believed the worst was over. One of those was Benjamin Graham, the father of security analysis, Warren Buffett's teacher and a great investor in his own right.

In 1930, Graham was 36 years old and a near millionaire and had already enjoyed a lot of success in markets. So, when he met with a successful, retired 93-year-old businessman named John Dix, Graham was full of "smug self-confidence," as he would admit in his memoir. Graham found Dix "surprisingly alert" as Dix peppered him with all kinds of questions. Then Dix asked him how much money Graham owed to banks. Dix didn't like what he heard.

That's because Graham used a lot of debt in his investment fund to finance stock purchases. When Dix heard this, he offered him a grave warning with "the greatest earnestness." Dix said,

> Mr. Graham, I want you to do something of the greatest importance to yourself. Get on the train to New York tomorrow; go to your office, sell out your securities; pay off your debts, and return the capital to your partners. I wouldn't be able to sleep one moment at night if I were in your position in these times, and you shouldn't be able to sleep either. I'm much older than you, with lots more experience, and you'd better take my advice.

Graham, of course, didn't take his advice. He even writes in his memoir that he "thanked the old man, a bit condescendingly no doubt."

Of course, Dix was right, and the worst was yet to come. "I have often wondered what my life would have been like it [sic] if I had followed his advice," Graham muses. Graham suffered mightily in 1930, his worst year ever:

	Benjamin Graham Joint Account	Dow Jones Industrials
1929	-20%	-15%
1930	-50%	-29%
1931	-16%	-48%
1932	-3%	-17%
For entire period	-70%	-74%

After 1930, he did unwind the debt he held in his account and he did much better thereafter in what was a mercilessly difficult market. Given that Graham's partnership had 44 percent of its assets financed by debt going into 1930, just pacing the market would have wiped him out. Irving Kahn, another great old investor and student of Graham's, wrote of Graham's ordeal in the 1930s, "Keeping the fund alive was a great achievement. The small losses of 1931 and 1932 were especially impressive."

Graham's big mistake was using too much debt. That's why Dix told him he shouldn't be able to sleep at night. Dix appreciated just how dangerous all that leverage was. The inspiration in Graham's tale, though, is that he fought his way back and went on to earn good returns in the market in later years.

The lesson he learned is a lesson we have to learn in every cycle, it seems.

CHAPTER 15:

100-BAGGERS DISTILLED: ESSENTIAL PRINCIPLES

Let's bring this back to where it began, with Charles Akre, whose speech "An Investor's Odyssey" set this Phelpsian quest in motion. (See chapter 1.) Akre has a couple of 100-baggers under his belt, and a lifetime of investing has taught him the key principle behind making 100 times your money.

While this book was in its final stages, I met Akre in his office, which is far away from the frenetic pace of Wall Street.

I drove down along the western edge of the Washington beltway. Then I headed west, deeper into Virginia. The urban landscape gave way to green fields and woods. I drove past wineries and horse farms and fieldstone fences, and past little towns with antiques shops and historic mills and churches.

Eventually, I came to Middleburg, a picturesque little town of about 600 people. Then, down a quiet side street, I found a nicely refurbished building that used to be a tavern but was now an office.

Here is where Charles T. Akre Jr. ("Chuck") has his HQ. It has a calm and comfortable feel to it, with bookshelves full of books and horse-themed art on the wall. I felt as if I was in someone's home.

Akre, 72, has been in the securities business since 1968. He's one of the great investors of our time. I have a bound volume of his letters to partners from 1993 to 2013, titled *The Power of Compounding*. A dollar invested with Akre turned into nearly $20, compared with just $5.59 for the S&P 500.

As I noted, it was a speech Akre gave in 2011 that introduced me to Thomas Phelps and his book *100 to 1 in the Stock Market*. Phelps's book is one of Akre's favorites. So I was glad to spend some time with him and members of his team—Tom Saberhagen, Chris Cerrone and Ben Fox. We went to lunch at the Red Fox Inn & Tavern, which has been around since 1728 and is only about 400 feet from his office.

Akre, as I mentioned, had a couple of 100-bagger stocks in his portfolio.

He bought Berkshire Hathaway stock back in 1977, paying $120 per share. Each share is now worth an astonishing 1,750 times what he paid. Here's a funny story about this. On my way out, Tom, who is a portfolio manager and partner of the firm, gave me that bound copy of Akre's letters. This is unputdownable reading for me. I love this kind of stuff and read these things like other people read novels.

In a 1995 letter, Akre tells the story of how when he was a young broker, he bought a share of Berkshire. He went on to accumulate about 40 shares. Then he decided in 1981 to get into real estate. He had a con-do-conversion project and needed the money. So he sold all his shares save one for $500 per share. Of course, that turned out to be one super expensive project. Those 39 shares—worth $19,500 back then—would be worth $8.1 million today.

The other 100-bagger is American Tower, spun off from American Radio back in 1998. Akre paid about 80 cents for each of his first shares, and they are now worth $93 per share. This stock he still had as of our meeting, and it was his largest position, according to filings.

Akre's approach is simple and easy to understand. He calls it his three-legged stool. He looks for

- businesses that have historically compounded value per share at very high rates;

- highly skilled managers who have a history of treating share-holders as though they are partners; and
- businesses that can reinvest their free cash flow in a manner that continues to earn above-average returns.

We've talked about all of these in this book.

As he told me, though, the older he gets, the more he whittles things down to the essentials. And the most essential thing is that third item. This is the most important principle behind the 100-bagger. In one of his letters, he puts it this way: "Over a period of years, our thinking has focused more and more on the issue of reinvestment as the single most critical ingredient in a successful investment idea, once you have already identified an outstanding business."

Consider a business with $100 invested in it. Say it earns a 20 percent return on its capital in one year. That is a high return and would get Akre interested. A 20 percent return implies $20 in earnings. But the key to a really great idea would be a business that could then take that $20 and reinvest it alongside the original $100 and earn a 20 percent return again and again and again.

As an aside, you'll note the absence of dividends. When a company pays a dividend, it has that much less capital to reinvest. Instead, you have it in your pocket—after paying taxes. Ideally, you want to find a company that can reinvest those dollars at a high rate. You wind up with a bigger pile at the end of the day and pay less in taxes.

To get back to the example, at the end of that first year, you would have $120. Soon after, the magic starts to happen:

1	$120.00	6	$298.60
2	$144.00	7	$358.32
3	$172.80	8	$429.98
4	$207.83	9	$515.98
5	$248.83	10	$619.17

At the end of the fourth year, you've doubled your money. At the end of 10 years, you've got a six-bagger. And in about 25 years, you'll have

100x your money. Of course, you don't have to hold for the whole time. And there is no guarantee a business can keep up such a pace. I'm just showing you the power of compounding.

Compounding is what lies at the heart of Akre's approach. He wants to find that great business and just sit tight—just like Phelps.

I'd also add that Akre runs a focused fund. His top five to seven ideas often make up half of his portfolio. This is something we've covered in chapter 10. The great investors concentrate on their best ideas.

At lunch, we just talked about businesses and stocks the whole time. Akre was cheerful and relaxed; he never checked his phone. He was full of wise words on investing, and funny too. He talked about Phelps and about 100-baggers. He talked about books read and lessons learned. This is the way great investors talk.

Believe me, I've met a bunch of them, from Ackman to Wanger. (Bill Ackman of Pershing Square fame you probably know. Ralph Wanger you may not. He ran the top-performing Acorn Fund for a lot of years and wrote a fine book about investing titled *A Zebra in Lion Country*.)

You might find it instructive what we didn't talk about:

- We didn't talk about the Fed.
- We didn't talk about the overall market.
- We didn't talk about the dollar.

Not that those things are unimportant. They are important. But they are unknowable and unpredictable things. And great investors don't spend a lot of time on them. They focus on trying to find those great opportunities—like Berkshire Hathaway and American Tower were for Akre. These stocks just overpowered all those big-picture concerns.

The Essential Principles of Finding 100-Baggers

The most important principle is the one identified above. It's so important it's worth repeating again: you need a business with a high return on capital with the ability to reinvest and earn that high return on capital for years and years.

Everything else is ancillary to this principle. Below are summaries of these other principles.

#1 You Have to Look for Them

Obvious? Maybe. But critically important.

It's why Phelps starts his book with a little parable about the four men granted a wish. The first guy asks for one donkey, which he gets. And the second man asks for 10 donkeys—which he gets. The idea is if you ask for one donkey, you get only one donkey. (And if you ask for 10 you'll never get more than 10.)

Phelps also uses an analogy from his experiences hunting for elephants in equatorial Africa. (Not very PC, I know. Different era.) "When looking for the biggest game, be not tempted to shoot at anything small."

So, rule number one for finding 100-baggers is that you have to look for them—and that means you don't bother playing the game for eighths and quarters, as the saying goes. Don't waste limited mental bandwidth on stocks that might pay a good yield or that might rise 30 percent or 50 percent.

You only have so much time and so many resources to devote to stock research. Focus your efforts on the big game: The elephants. The 100-baggers.

#2 Growth, Growth and More Growth

There is no way around it. Almost all of the businesses in the 100-bagger study were substantially bigger businesses at the end than when they began. (There is an exception to this, which I'll highlight below.)

So, you need growth—and lots of it. But not just any growth. You want value-added growth. You want "good growth." If a company doubles its sales, but also doubles the shares outstanding, that's no good. You want to focus on growth in sales and earnings per share.

Likewise, if a company generates a lot of extra sales by cutting its prices and driving down its return on equity, that may not be the kind of growth you're looking for. You want to find a business that has lots of room to expand—it's what drives those reinvestment opportunities.

And yes, I'm being intentionally vague about whether you want sales growth or earnings growth. You'd love both. But there are also examples of 100-baggers that grew sales at a high rate but did not show much in the way of reported earnings through the high-growth phase. (Comcast and Amazon are examples we covered.)

Earnings are the reported numbers, whatever they are. Earnings power, however, reflects the ability of the stock to earn above-average rates of return on capital at above-average growth rates. It's essentially a longer-term assessment of competitive strengths.

This is a distinction Phelps makes in his book *100 to 1 in the Stock Market*. He writes, "Failure to distinguish between ephemeral earnings fluctuations and basic changes in earnings power accounts for much over trading, [and] many lost opportunities to make 100 for one in the stock market."

Don't get lost following earnings per share on a quarterly basis. Even one year may not be long enough to judge. It is more important to think about earnings power. A company can report a fall in earnings, but its longer-term earnings power could be unaffected. In the same way, earnings may rise but the underlying earnings power may be weakening. For example, a company might have great earnings but a high percentage may come from one-off sources.

So, how do you separate the ephemeral earnings setback from the real thing? Well, there is no substitute for knowing the business you've invested in. If you don't understand what you own, it's impossible to make a wise choice. Let me illustrate by way of an example.

There is a business I like called General Finance (GFN). It's a simple business. It leases containers—the kind of things you see on construction sites where people store things.

In addition to these, GFN leases

- freight containers—used by road and rail operators—which can store dry bulk goods and refrigerated goods;
- portable building containers—essentially mobile mini-offices or lunchrooms, first aid rooms, and so on—used by construction firms and natural-resource companies and even for public events;

- portable liquid tank containers—which can hold wastewater, chemicals and other liquids—used in oil and gas, environmental remediation and the like; and
- mobile offices and modular buildings.

The economics of container leasing are fantastic. Payback is only a few years, but the asset has a 40-year life. So, we're talking about high returns on capital. The industry is fragmented, and there is lots of room to grow by acquiring mom-and-pop operations. And there is a talented and proven owner-operator in Ron Valenta.

In early 2015, the stock sells off hard on earnings slowing down because of a slowdown in oil and gas sales. GFN leases containers to oil and gas customers. But really, has the earnings power of GFN been compromised in any way? Is the long-term thesis here cancelled out because of a slowdown?

The answer is no.

They still have their containers, which they can lease elsewhere. GFN has a fleet of about 37,000 storage containers. Its customer list is diverse. GFN serves over 30,000 customers across 20 industries. These assets didn't go anywhere.

They still generate tons of cash. There are still a lot of mom-and-pop operations out there they can continue to roll up. As Valenta put it in an interview with me,

> We probably spend as much time or more time on a company once we acquire it. We have great product breadth, so we can make improvements there. We look at billing systems. Are they billing monthly or every 28 days? Do they have damage waivers? How are they handling trucking? So we analyze the business and what can we do with it. . . . We're not just an acquirer. What we're really good at it is taking things and improving on them dramatically. We're a very disciplined buyer. *But more importantly, we're a value creator in what we do with the asset.* (emphasis added)

That hasn't changed. All that's changed is a temporary dip in earnings because of a cyclical change in fortunes in its customer base. There is no new competitive threat. There was no management change. There is no new regulation or other factor that might change this business in any significant way.

This is the kind of thinking I do. As you can tell, you can only do this if you know the business well. Spend less time reading economic forecasters and stock market prognosticators, and spend more time on understanding what you own. If you're not willing to do it, then you're not going to net a 100-bagger or anything close to it.

#3 Lower Multiples Preferred

You don't want to pay stupid prices.

Let's say you pay 50 times earnings for a company that generated $1 in earnings last year. Think what you need to happen to make it a 100-bagger. You need earnings to go up a hundredfold *and* you need the price–earnings ratio to stay where it is at 50. If the price–earnings ratio falls to 25, then you need earnings to rise 200-fold.

Don't make investing so hard.

We saw earlier in our case study of Gillette how a price–earning ratio collapse from 20 to 10 blunted the return investors got from Gillette's earnings growth.

But on the other hand, you shouldn't go dumpster diving if you want to turn up 100-baggers. Great stocks have a ready fan club, and many will spend most of their time near their 52-week highs, as you'd expect. It is rare to get a truly great business at dirt-cheap prices. If you spend your time trolling stocks with price–earnings ratios of five or trading at deep discounts to book value or the like, you're hunting in the wrong fields—at least as far as 100-baggers go. You may get lucky there, of course, but the targets are richer in less austere settings.

I say lower multiples "preferred" because you can't draw hard rules about any of this stuff. There are times when even 50 times earnings is a bargain. You have to balance the price you pay against other factors.

Remember, time is the friend of the great business. And you can pay more for a great business. Let me give you another example: Interactive Brokers (IBKR), the online broker.

Matthew Goodman (the analyst who did the case study on Monster Beverage) did an analysis of IBKR, a stock we recommended in our newsletter. He showed how it has been applying new technology to an age-old business. Its platform is more capable than competitors and it is easily the least-cost option.

You can see this anecdotally in industry news, as Goodman points out:

- According to legendary trader Peter Brandt, talking about Interactive Brokers, "On one trading platform and with one account I can trade the world—from US to global futures markets, US and global stock exchanges, options, forex, you name it. . . . Credit Suisse would offer me the same package for an account worth $50 million. Ditto for Goldman and D-Bank. No other firms I know of provide this capability for accounts under $5–10 million."
- Bank of America, JPMorgan and others are giving their hedge fund clients the boot. Some, like E-Trade, are closing global trading accounts. Where do these customers all go? Interactive Brokers.
- Scottrade recently added its clients to IBKR's platform. Scottrade is a competitor, and it's essentially put up the white flag.

Goodman writes you can also see all of this in the numbers. He showed how growth in new accounts was actually accelerating at IBKR:

Interactive brokers electronic brokerage statistics

	2015	% Change		
	Apr	Pr Mo	Pr Yr	Pr Mo Ann
(in 000's)				
Total Accounts	302.0	2%	18%	23%
Net New Accounts	5.6	-16%	40%	
(in Billions)				
Client Equity	$65.2	7%	32%	780%
Client Credits	$33.6	6%	24%	68%
Client Margin Loans	$8.7	8%	27%	97%

"This is information one can find in the IR section of the IBKR website," Goodman wrote. "I added the last column, 'Prior month annualized.'" Key takeaways here: While year-over-year growth seems impressive, month-over-month growth is even more impressive. And client equity is growing even faster than total accounts. That's a huge positive trend because it means the business is attracting wealthier customers who are opening larger accounts."

So, this is a fast-growing business. But the stock traded for about 25 times earnings in late 2014, when you backed out the excess capital it had. That is not a low multiple. So was it worth it?

Charlie Munger, vice chairman of Berkshire Hathaway said,

> Over the long term, it's hard for a stock to earn a much better return than the business which underlies it earns. If the business earns 6% on capital over 40 years and you hold it for that 40 years, you're not going to make much different than a 6% return—even if you originally buy it at a huge discount. Conversely, if a business earns 18% on capital over 20 or 30 years, even if you pay an expensive looking price, you'll end up with a fine result.

"That quote is a cornerstone of a 100-bagger philosophy," Goodman wrote. (And it's the second time we've referred to the quote in this book.) "We're looking for companies with very high returns on capital. That's one of the key requirements 100-baggers must meet. And this quote proves the point. Here's a table to breathe some life into Munger's comment."

You can see how dramatically different a 6 percent return is from an 18 percent return.

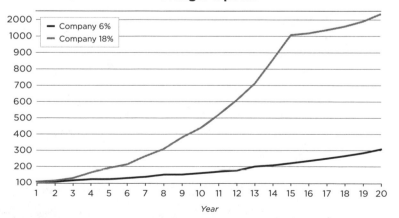

Munger's point

At the end of 20 years, a company returning 18 percent on capital winds up with a pile nearly eight times larger. The lesson: don't miss out on the chance to acquire great businesses at fair prices, and you can clearly see why in this chart.

"One way to look at it is by using something called the PEG ratio," Goodman suggests. "The PEG ratio is simply the (P/E Ratio)/(Annual EPS Growth Rate). If earnings grow 20%, for example, then a P/E of 20 is justified. Anything too far above 1x could be too expensive."

IBKR's brokerage pretax earning growth rates for 2010–2014 were 19 percent, 35 percent, -8 percent, 33 percent and 29 percent. IBKR's earnings grew 29 percent in 2014, yet the stock traded at 26 times earnings, giving us a PEG under one—unusual for such a high-quality business growing quickly in today's market. The fact that we can get it under one is a major plus.

Again, this is an example of the kind of thinking you should work through. Just remember that the higher the multiple you pay, the higher the earnings growth rate needs to be.

To repeat once more: lower multiples preferred.

#2 and #3 Together
Get What I Call the Twin Engines of a 100-Bagger

When you get lots of growth and a low multiple you get the twin engine of 100-baggers. That's where you really get some great lift, with both factors working in your favor.

Earlier in the book, we went through the extreme example of MTY Foods. There we had a stock start at 3.5 times earnings. Earnings rose 12.4 times in 10 years, but the stock was a 100-bagger because the price–earnings ratio went from 3.5 to 27. You should know that's rare, but it makes the point rather well.

#4 Economic Moats Are a Necessity

A 100-bagger requires a high return on capital for a long time. A moat, by definition, is what allows a company to get that return. Therefore, it pays to spend some time thinking about what kind of moat a company has.

There's a whole chapter on this, so I won't repeat the lessons here. I'll just add some basic math about the importance of earning a high return on capital and—you can't forget this second part—the ability to reinvest at high rates for years on end.

Phelps walks through an example in his book that is worth repeating here. Assume a company has $10 per share in book value and earns 15 percent on that capital. At the end of one year, book value will be $11.50 per share, if the stock pays no dividend. At the end of the second year, it will be $13.22, and at the end of the third year $15.20.

"In five years, the company's book value will have doubled," Phelps writes. "In 10 years, it will have quadrupled. In 33 years, it will be up one hundredfold."

If the company had paid dividends, the story would be quite different. Say it paid out one-third of its earnings. It would then take 15 years to quadruple its capital, not 10. And in 33 years, it would be up 23-fold, instead of being a 100-bagger.

"Obviously," Phelps concludes, "dividends are an expensive luxury for an investor seeking maximum growth. If you must have income, don't expect your financial doctor to match the capital gains that might have been obtainable without dividends. When you buy a cow to milk, don't plan to race her against your neighbor's horse."

We saw this same view of dividends with Akre. There is a place for dividends, though, and they have been important to the overall return of many 100-baggers. However, we should prefer a company that can reinvest all of its earnings at a high clip. If it pays a dividend, that's less capital that it has to reinvest. And that reduces the rate of return.

If dividends are a drag, borrowed money is an accelerant. A company that earns 15 percent on its capital could raise it to, say, 20 percent by taking on some debt. But this raises the risk of the stock too.

There are other ways to net a 100-bagger. Discoveries of natural resources, such as a great new oil field, can get you a 100-bagger. New inventions and new blockbuster drugs can do the same. But these are hard to predict. So I would instead emphasize looking for high returns on capital and the ability to reinvest and produce high returns for years and years.

A moat, even a narrow moat, is a necessity.

#5 Smaller Companies Preferred

Start with acorns, wind up with oak trees. Start with oak trees, and you won't have quite the same dramatic growth. It may seem obvious, but it's important.

Apple, as great as it has been and is, won't become a 100-bagger from current levels. The market values the stock at $750 billion. A hundredfold return from here would take it to $75 trillion. That's more than four times the size of the US economy. It could be a good stock for some time yet, but the law of large numbers starts to work against you at some point.

On the other hand, you shouldn't assume you need to dive into micro-caps and buy 25-cent stocks. The median sales figure of the 365 names in the study was about $170 million. This is unadjusted for inflation. It simply shows you that 100-baggers can start off as sizable companies. Sales of $170 million makes for a substantial business in any era.

As a general rule, I suggest focusing on companies with market caps of less than $1 billion. Not a necessity (remember, smaller companies "preferred"), but staying below such a deck will make for a more fruitful search than staying above it.

#6 Owner-Operators Preferred

We spent a whole chapter on this idea. Many of the greatest businesses of the last 50 years had a human face behind them—an owner with vision and tenacity and skill: Sam Walton at Walmart. Steve Jobs at Apple. Jeff Bezos at Amazon. Warren Buffett at Berkshire Hathaway. The list is fairly long and we've mentioned several of them in prior chapters.

Having a great owner-operator also adds to your conviction. I find it easier to hold onto a stock through the rough patches knowing I have a talented owner-operator with skin in the game at the helm.

I would also remind you of something you should never forget: No one creates a stock so you can make money. Every stock is available to you only because somebody wanted to sell it.

Thinking about that in the abstract, there seems to be no reason why you should expect to make money in a stock. But investing with owner-operators is a good reason to think you will. Because then you become a partner. You invest your money in the same securities the people who control the business own. What's good for them is good for you. And vice versa.

It's not perfect, but it's often better than investing with management that aren't owners. It helps solve the age-old agency problem. Seek out and prefer owner-operators.

It's preferred, but not required. There are also businesses for which it would be hard to name a CEO. Gillette was a 100-bagger in our study's time period (1962–2014). And yet I am hard pressed to name its CEO or any of its CEOs. And companies do outlive and outrun their founders and owner-operators.

#7 You Need Time: Use the Coffee-Can Approach as a Crutch

Once you do all this work to find a stock that could become a 100-bagger, you need to give it time. Even the fastest 100-baggers in our study needed about five years to get there. A more likely journey will take 20–25 years.

Knowing this, you need to find a way to defeat your own worst instincts—the impatience, the need for "action," the powerful feeling that you need to "do something." To defeat this baleful tendency, I offer you the coffee can as a crutch. I'm a big fan of the coffee-can approach, and we spent a whole chapter exploring the idea.

The genius of the technique lies in its simplicity. You take some portion of your money and create a "coffee-can portfolio." What you put in it, you commit to holding for 10 years. That's it.

At the end of 10 years, you see what you have. Coffee-can experience says you will have found at least one big winner in there. Coffee-can theory says you'll have done better this way than if you had tried to more actively manage your stocks.

You may dismiss this as gimmicky. But I urge you to find some way to leave your stocks alone. Let them ripen on the vines. Don't pick them too early.

#8 You Need a Really Good Filter

There is a world of noise out there. The financial media is particularly bad. Every day, something important happens, or so they would have you believe. They narrate every twist in the market. They cover every Fed meeting. They document the endless stream of economic data and reports. They give a platform for an unending parade of pundits. Everybody wants to try to call the market, or predict where interest rates will go or the price of oil or whatever.

My own study of 100-baggers shows what a pathetic waste of time this all is. It's a great distraction in your hunt for 100-baggers.

To get over this, you have to first understand that stock prices move for all kinds of reasons. Sometimes stocks make huge moves in a month, up or down, and yet the business itself changes more slowly over time.

There are great examples of this all over the place. Because it's at hand, I'll share a snapshot my analyst Matt Goodman forwarded to me about Monster Beverage, a 100-bagger we covered earlier.

It's a sort of "heat map" and shows you the monthly moves Monster's stock made each month from 2000 to 2014. On the far right-hand side, you'll see the annual move.

Just look at this chart on the next two pages for a bit and see what jumps out at you.

	JAN	FEB	MAR	Q1	APR	MAY	JUNE	Q2
2015	7.94%	20.67%	-1.93%	27.73%	-0.93%	-7.17%	5.30%	-3.16%
2014	0.19%	8.98%	-6.15%	2.48%	-3.59%	3.61%	2.38%	2.28%
2013	-9.35%	5.34%	-5.39%	-9.65%	18.14%	-3.21%	11.43%	27.42%
2012	13.44%	9.41%	8.59%	34.77%	4.69%	11.69%	-1.93%	14.67%
2011	8.34%	1.59%	4.66%	15.19%	9.86%	8.31%	12.98%	34.44%
2010	0.16%	8.11%	4.33%	12.97%	1.75%	-11.55%	0.15%	-9.87%
2009	-0.12%	-0.66%	8.17%	7.33%	13.22%	-10.01%	-15.87%	-14.28%
2008	-12.92%	7.62%	-14.94%	-20.28%	0.28%	-11.75%	-7.75%	-18.36%
2007	13.12%	-8.14%	8.23%	12.47%	0.84%	4.19%	7.99%	13.46%
2006	11.37%	6.38%	35.05%	60.00%	2.66%	42.83%	2.99%	51.02%
2005	12.78%	6.64%	37.36%	65.20%	-5.60%	31.64%	13.52%	41.07%
2004	5.66%	32.14%	18.92%	66.04%	-1.14%	89.66%	-4.24%	79.55%
2003	0.00%	-3.70%	3.85%	0.00%	-3.70%	3.85%	0.00%	0.00%
2002	-3.70%	0.00%	3.85%	0.00%	-3.70%	3.85%	0.00%	0.00%
2001	8.33%	-11.54%	-8.70%	-12.50%	-4.76%	0.00%	5.00%	0.00%
2000	3.70%	-7.14%	7.69%	0.00%	0.00%	-3.57%	-3.70%	-7.14%

Source: Sentieo

JULY	AUG	SEPT	Q3	OCT	NOV	DEC	Q4	Y
3.14%			3.14%					27.58%
-9.95%	38.23%	3.69%	29.06%	10.05%	11.17%	-3.39%	18.20%	59.88%
0.26%	-5.90%	-8.96%	-14.10%	9.53%	3.41%	14.52%	29.70%	28.26%
-6.71%	-11.26%	-8.28%	-24.07%	-17.41%	16.57%	1.52%	-2.26%	14.70%
-5.36%	11.35%	2.32%	7.83%	2.06%	3.48%	-0.07%	5.54%	76.24%
7.16%	7.49%	3.51%	19.23%	9.87%	3.90%	-1.77%	12.14%	36.15%
0.52%	5.29%	12.49%	19.05%	-1.63%	-3.27%	9.84%	4.52%	14.19%
-20.68%	20.21%	10.12%	5.00%	-16.33%	17.54%	12.70%	10.84%	-24.25%
-5.60%	10.75%	26.24%	31.88%	19.97%	-36.18%	2.03%	-21.88%	31.47%
-3.36%	-40.13%	17.94%	-31.76%	-2.22%	-11.46%	19.77%	3.69%	70.96%
9.26%	7.44%	-5.31%	11.15%	7.48%	53.64%	1.44%	67.52%	333.92%
-18.99%	16.41%	1.34%	-4.43%	9.93%	27.11%	7.58%	50.33%	328.30%
18.52%	15.62%	-2.70%	33.33%	16.67%	33.33%	-5.36%	47.22%	96.30%
-3.70%	0.00%	0.00%	-3.70%	3.85%	0.00%	0.00%	3.85%	0.00%
14.29%	0.00%	-8.33%	4.76%	9.09%	4.17%	8.00%	22.73%	12.50%
7.69%	14.29%	6.25%	30.77%	0.00%	-32.35%	4.35%	-29.41%	-14.29%

It's incredible. You see months where the stock lost 20 percent in a month, a few where it lost even more. And you see months where the stock jumped 20 percent or more. In at least a few instances, these moves were back to back.

Now, you know the business of Monster did not change anything like that much in any of those months. We're talking about a maker of beverages. You can also see on the far right-hand side that even with all the movement, the stock marched up and to the right most of the time.

Think about all those times, however, when the stock took a 20+ percent dive. How often would you have been watching it, day after day? How likely is it you would have sold it? Maybe after a 20 percent drop, you'd have decided to get out at the next opportunity. Then you'd have sold after a good month.

All that intense watching and hand-wringing would have been a waste of time. The attempt to trade it would have been a mistake. Monster was a fantastic stock and you should have left it alone.

Another temptation is to get too concerned over where the stock market is going.

The big-picture crowd loves to analyze stock market indices, such as the S&P 500. They love to cite CAPE ratios (price divided by an average of the past 10 years of earnings) and other metrics to divine the path of future returns.

Just because a stock market index, such as the S&P 500, is pricey doesn't mean you should give up on stocks. Unless you are a buyer of the index itself, it is not relevant to the business of finding great stocks today.

Let me give you a historical example: 1966 to 1982.

The big-picture crowd likes to cite this 17-year stretch as dead money for stocks. The Dow Jones Industrial Average basically went nowhere. (This performance was worse than it appears because inflation was high during this period.) Thus, you might conclude, you didn't want to be in stocks.

But here's what my research on stocks that returned 100 to 1 found: there were 187 stocks you could've bought between 1966 and 1982 that would have multiplied your money 100x.

In fact, during that 17-year stretch, you'd have had at least a dozen opportunities each month to multiply your money 100x if you just held on. In some cases, you didn't even have to wait very long. Southwest Airlines returned more than 100x in about 10 years beginning in 1971. Leslie Wexler's L Brands did it in about 8 years starting in 1978. In 1966, you could've bought H&R Block and turned a $10,000 investment into $1 million in under two decades.

The indices can tell you what kind of environment you are in. It's certainly harder to find great opportunities in highly priced markets. And it's easier to find big winners at market bottoms (but perhaps not so easy to make yourself buy them, as fear is rife at such times). These facts should surprise no one.

My point is, don't fret so much with guesses as to where the stock market might go. Keep looking for great ideas. If history is any guide, they are always out there.

As I say, you need a really good filter.

#9 Luck Helps

Let's face it. There is an element of luck in all of this.

No one could've predicted back in 2002 what Apple would become. No one could've predicted they'd invent whole new markets—the iPod, the iPad, the iPhone. There are some 100-baggers in this study where I just threw up my hands, resigned to the fact that they were unpredictable.

Likewise, bad things happen. You could do all the work right, and then, some new innovation comes along that crosses what seemed an impregnable moat. Just look at how many businesses have been destroyed or severely impaired in recent times—video rentals, newspapers, the music industry, even taxis.

I quote here from Nicholas Rescher's elegant meditation on chance, *Luck: The Brilliant Randomness of Everyday Life*:

> To be sure, given our natural human commitment to the idea that we live in a rational world, we are inclined to think that there is always an ultimate reason. . . . All of this is perfectly natural but

also totally futile. The only ultimately rational attitude is to sit loosely in the saddle of life and to come to terms with the idea of chance as such.

Just as in life, so in the pursuit of 100-baggers. Good luck helps.

#10 You Should Be a Reluctant Seller

So, when do you sell?

In his book *Common Stocks and Uncommon Profits*, Phil Fisher had a chapter called "When to Sell." He summed it up this way: "Perhaps the thoughts behind this chapter might be put in a single sentence: If the job has been correctly done when a common stock is purchased, the time to sell it is—almost never."

That is probably right. There are certainly many examples where this philosophy in action resulted in riches beyond what seemed possible at the time of purchase.

On never selling, I think of the Astor family fortune. John Jacob Astor was the patriarch, and when he died in 1848, he was America's wealthiest man. The estate passed to his son, William Astor. He grew the family fortune even further.

There is a piece of testimony, on some tax matter, before the New York Senate Committee in 1890. I love this bit of dialogue (which I included in my first book *Invest Like a Dealmaker*):

Q: You have just said that Mr. Astor never sold?

A: Once in a while he sells, yes.

Q: But the rule is that he does not sell?

A: Well, hardly ever. He has sold, of course.

Q: Isn't it almost a saying in this community that the Astors buy and never sell?

A: They are not looked upon as people who dispose of real estate after they once get possession of it.

As I wrote in *Dealmaker*, "The key to the great Astor fortune—what gave it staying power and allowed it to multiply to such extraordinary heights—was the simple fact that the Astors were reluctant sellers. Once they got hold of a good thing, they held on and allowed the magic of compounding to do its work."

One more anecdotal example from today: Ronald Read.

Anna Prior wrote a wonderful story about him for the *Wall Street Journal*. The headline was "The Frugal Man Who Left an $8 Million Estate."

Ronald Read was a janitor at JC Penney "after a long stint at a service station that was owned in part by his brother." So how did he make his money? He was a good stock picker. But more important, he was patient.

He had 95 stocks when he died. Many of these he held for decades. He owned pieces of a variety of sectors but avoided technology. When he got dividends, he used them to buy more shares. He owned Procter & Gamble, JP Morgan, JM Smucker, Johnson & Johnson and other blue chips. Not every stock he owned was a winner. But the profits from the winners overwhelmed the losers.

Read also physically held his stock certificates. This had to make it easier to hold onto his stocks. They became more real, like a piece of property instead of just a glowing stock-ticker symbol that existed on computer screens.

Fees eventually made it impractical to hold certificates, so he switched to having his shares held by the official record keeper of share ownership (called the transfer agent) that each company employs. This is a thrifty option and the record shows Read paid very low fees.

The story of Ronald Read shows you the power of simple investing concepts: keeping fees low, investing in quality companies, reinvesting dividends and—most importantly for our purposes—the power of just holding on.

So, you can certainly make a case for "almost never."

But even Fisher allows there are reasons to sell:

- You've made a mistake—that is, "the factual background of the particular company is less favorable than originally believed."
- The stock no longer meets your investment criteria.

- You want to switch into something better—although an investor should be careful here and only switch if "very sure of his ground."

Looking at those, you can see that the decision of when to sell is still not easy. It's not so easy to know when you've made a mistake. You can certainly talk yourself into believing anything. The second one is maybe the easiest, if you have well-defined investment criteria. Finally, switching is treacherous too. Every stock that's moving looks better than the one you're thinking of selling. And there are always stocks that are moving.

You'll note that none of these reasons has anything to do with the stock price.

In his *100 to 1 in the Stock Market*, Thomas Phelps too is a great proponent of buying right and holding on. But "does this mean one should never sell anything?" he asks. The answer is no.

Phelps's selling advice is one you can sum up in one sentence too: "Never if you can help it take an investment action for a non-investment reason."

Some of these "non-investment reasons" include these:

1. My stock is "too high."
2. I need the realized capital gain to offset realized capital losses for tax purposes.
3. My stock is not moving. Others are.

Phelps believes you should sell when you've made a mistake. And once again, as with all great investors, he does not define a mistake as a stock that is simply down in price. (In fact, in a bull market, a mistake may well mean taking profits. It's a mistake because it represents a lost opportunity to have made bigger profits. And you pay a capital gains tax as a penalty.)

I know a lot of people use so-called "stop losses." This is when you sell a stock once it's fallen a certain amount. Stop losses are popular because they take a difficult decision—perhaps the most difficult in all of investing—and make it mechanical. You don't have to think about it. The stock hit your stop loss and you are out.

It should be apparent that it also limits your ability to net a 100-bagger.

You would've been stopped out of every one long before it ever returned 100 to 1.

Monster Beverage became a 100-bagger in 10 years, as we've seen. Remember the heat map above? I count at least 10 different occasions where it fell more than 25 percent during that run. In three separate months, it lost more than 40 percent of its value. Yet if you focused on the business—and not the stock price—you would never have sold. And if you put $10,000 in that stock, you would have $1 million at the end of 10 years.

I have many such examples. It's true you could get lucky and hit a double or triple by getting the timing right on something. But in that effort, you'll surely be stopped out of a lot of ideas along the way. And what is the point of going through all the research required to come up with an idea if you're going to let your neighbor dictate your sell price?

Second, you might say to yourself, "Well, I can buy it back later." But honestly, will you buy it back? I think it is easier to say these things than to do them. Investing is such a mental game.

Further, you might point to periods where stocks got bubbly. In 1998 or 1999, Coke was trading for 50 times earnings. It was a sell then. But then again, would Coke have qualified for a buy based on our 100-bagger principles? I don't think so. It was a sell even by those lights.

Of course, investing in the buy-and-hold manner means sometimes you will be hit with a nasty loss. But that is why you own a portfolio of stocks. To me, investing in stocks is interesting only because you can make so much on a single stock. To truncate that upside because you are afraid to lose is like spending a lot of money on a car but never taking it out of the garage.

I invest in stocks knowing I could lose big on any position. Overall, though, I know I will turn in an excellent result.

I here quote again that wise old bird, Mr. Phelps. He writes, "Let us fall back on the principle that when any rule or formula become a substitute for thought rather than an aid to thinking, it is dangerous and should be discarded."

(A professor wrote in to tell me the above was a "self-negating rule." I suppose it is. Well, life is full of contradictions.)

Stop losses are a substitute for thought. What I present above are aids to thinking about the problem.

If there is one general principle, it is this: if you've done the job right and bought a stock only after careful study, then you should be a reluctant seller. I'll end this section on when to sell with one of my favorite quotes, from Martin Whitman at Third Avenue Funds: "I've been in this business for over fifty years. I have had a lot of experience holding stocks for three years; doubled, and I sold it for somebody else, for whom it tripled in the next six months. You make more money sitting on your ass."

If you are hunting for 100-baggers, you must learn to sit on your ass. Buy right and sit tight.

Coda: There Is No Magic Formula

By now, you've figured out there is no magic formula for producing 100-baggers. There is no easy way to screen for them. Still, in this final chapter, I've distilled things down to essential principles. Keep it handy and refer back often in your quest for 100-baggers.

I wish you good fortune and many 100-baggers in your own investing pursuits. And I hope this little book contributes in some small way to your successes.

APPENDIX

THE 100-BAGGERS (1962–2014)

	Data Date	Total Return	Years to 100
CAMPBELL SOUP CO	10/31/62	150	34.5
DEERE & CO	10/31/62	449	35.0
HEWLETT-PACKARD CO	10/31/62	498	30.7
HORMEL FOODS CORP	10/31/62	2,330	26.7
HOST HOTELS & RESORTS INC	10/31/62	844	22.4
MAY DEPARTMENT STORES CO	10/31/62	135	35.7
NORTHROP GRUMMAN CORP	10/31/62	907	31.4
ROLLINS INC	10/31/62	3,515	23.4
SEAGRAM CO LTD	10/31/62	171	33.3
TJX COMPANIES INC	10/31/62	6,946	28.5
GENERAL MILLS INC	11/30/62	869	28.7
LOEWS CORP	11/30/62	3,978	18.3
SHERWIN-WILLIAMS CO	11/30/62	894	41.6
ABBOTT LABORATORIES	12/31/62	1,965	27.7
ALCAN INC	12/31/62	126	45.0
ALLETE INC	12/31/62	259	41.3
ALTRIA GROUP INC	12/31/62	15,120	24.0
AMP INC	12/31/62	198	30.3
ANHEUSER-BUSCH COS INC	12/31/62	997	27.0

	Data Date	Total Return	Years to 100
BAXTER INTERNATIONAL INC	12/31/62	656	33.3
BEAM INC	12/31/62	391	33.5
BRISTOL-MYERS SQUIBB CO	12/31/62	616	33.5
CATERPILLAR INC	12/31/62	261	42.3
CHEVRON CORP	12/31/62	413	37.0
COCA-COLA CO	12/31/62	868	29.3
COLGATE-PALMOLIVE CO	12/31/62	814	34.8
COMERICA INC	12/31/62	365	33.3
COOPER INDUSTRIES PLC	12/31/62	537	28.7
CORESTATES FINANCIAL CORP	12/31/62	209	34.5
CRANE CO	12/31/62	1,158	27.0
CUMMINS INC	12/31/62	222	48.3
CVS HEALTH CORP	12/31/62	2,869	22.2
DISNEY (WALT) CO	12/31/62	3,276	23.7
DOW CHEMICAL	12/31/62	208	37.0
DPL INC	12/31/62	137	44.5
EATON CORP PLC	12/31/62	573	34.7
ECOLAB INC	12/31/62	2,074	33.3
EDISON INTERNATIONAL	12/31/62	183	43.3
EMERSON ELECTRIC CO	12/31/62	458	34.0
ENTERGY CORP	12/31/62	108	45.5
EXXON MOBIL CORP	12/31/62	637	34.5
FIRST CHICAGO NBD CORP	12/31/62	210	34.3
FIRSTAR CORP-OLD	12/31/62	251	33.8
GENERAL ELECTRIC CO	12/31/62	210	35.0
GILLETTE CO	12/31/62	221	31.7
GRACE (W R) & CO	12/31/62	209	49.0
GREAT PLAINS ENERGY INC	12/31/62	105	52.5
HALLIBURTON CO	12/31/62	290	35.0
HILLSHIRE BRANDS CO	12/31/62	942	28.8
HILTON WORLDWIDE HOLDINGS	12/31/62	763	21.2
IDACORP INC	12/31/62	117	52.0
INGERSOLL-RAND PLC	12/31/62	236	42.3
INTEGRYS ENERGY GROUP INC	12/31/62	268	42.5
INTL FLAVORS & FRAGRANCES	12/31/62	773	28.5

	Data Date	Total Return	Years to 100
ITT CORP	12/31/62	270	41.8
JPMORGAN CHASE & CO	12/31/62	128	51.0
KELLOGG CO	12/31/62	469	29.0
KROGER CO	12/31/62	1,222	28.5
MDU RESOURCES GROUP INC	12/31/62	221	38.8
MERCK & CO	12/31/62	826	28.8
MOBIL CORP	12/31/62	222	33.5
NEWMARKET CORP	12/31/62	5,077	22.8
OCCIDENTAL PETROLEUM CORP	12/31/62	464	41.8
OGE ENERGY CORP	12/31/62	216	47.8
PEPSICO INC	12/31/62	1,050	28.5
PERKINELMER INC	12/31/62	233	37.8
PFIZER INC	12/31/62	508	33.5
PHARMACIA CORP	12/31/62	116	35.5
PNC FINANCIAL SVCS GROUP INC	12/31/62	397	34.8
PROCTER & GAMBLE CO	12/31/62	399	34.7
QUAKER OATS CO	12/31/62	208	35.0
RAYTHEON CO	12/31/62	616	29.2
ROHM AND HAAS CO	12/31/62	126	44.8
ROYAL DUTCH PETROLEUM NV	12/31/62	456	30.3
SCHERING-PLOUGH	12/31/62	672	28.5
STANLEY BLACK & DECKER INC	12/31/62	590	33.8
SUNDSTRAND CORP	12/31/62	188	33.8
TEXAS INSTRUMENTS INC	12/31/62	428	34.5
TIMES MIRROR CO -SER A	12/31/62	206	34.3
UNITED TECHNOLOGIES CORP	12/31/62	687	35.8
UST INC	12/31/62	2,293	26.0
VULCAN MATERIALS CO	12/31/62	979	25.3
WARNER-LAMBERT CO	12/31/62	370	34.5
WELLS FARGO & CO	12/31/62	952	34.3
WHIRLPOOL CORP	12/31/62	480	35.3
WISCONSIN ENERGY CORP	12/31/62	357	43.0
WRIGLEY (WM) JR CO	12/31/62	760	30.0
WYETH	12/31/62	215	33.8
XCEL ENERGY INC	12/31/62	123	51.8

	Data Date	Total Return	Years to 100
KIMBERLY-CLARK CORP	10/31/63	498	31.2
3M CO	12/31/63	199	46.2
AIR PRODUCTS & CHEMICALS INC	12/31/63	579	33.2
BECTON DICKINSON & CO	12/31/63	501	34.0
JOHNSON & JOHNSON	12/31/63	1,459	28.8
PPG INDUSTRIES INC	12/31/63	701	33.5
HEINZ (H J) CO	10/31/64	639	25.3
MEADWESTVACO CORP	10/31/64	123	49.2
ASHLAND INC	12/31/64	182	48.0
DUN & BRADSTREET CORP	12/31/64	684	34.3
SUNOCO INC	12/31/64	102	41.5
UNILEVER NV	12/31/64	856	27.3
BERKSHIRE HATHAWAY	9/30/65	18,261	19.0
ONEOK INC	11/30/65	473	39.1
ALLIANT ENERGY CORP	12/31/65	169	45.3
EQT CORP	12/31/65	713	34.0
KINDER MORGAN INC	12/31/65	739	29.3
MCDONALD'S CORP	12/31/65	3,983	18.7
SEMPRA ENERGY	12/31/65	138	47.0
WESTAR ENERGY INC	12/31/65	106	48.3
BLOCK H & R INC	10/31/66	2,873	19.5
HOLLYFRONTIER CORP	10/31/66	12,279	21.2
ARCHER-DANIELS-MIDLAND CO	12/31/66	678	25.3
AUTOMATIC DATA PROCESSING	12/31/66	2,728	21.5
BARD (C.R.) INC	12/31/66	445	37.2
DOVER CORP	12/31/66	1,148	26.3
FIRST HORIZON NATIONAL CORP	12/31/66	125	30.5
GENUINE PARTS CO	12/31/66	737	29.2
HELMERICH & PAYNE	12/31/66	648	31.0
KENNAMETAL INC	12/31/66	119	41.5
MARSH & MCLENNAN COS	12/31/66	500	31.0
NORTHERN TRUST CORP	12/31/66	418	31.3
VF CORP	12/31/66	2,298	26.0
HARCOURT GENERAL INC	10/31/67	615	18.3
LOWE'S COMPANIES INC	10/31/67	1,958	26.5

	Data Date	Total Return	Years to 100
AVERY DENNISON CORP	11/30/67	191	31.3
SUNAMERICA INC	11/30/67	2,733	23.3
AMERICAN EXPRESS CO	12/31/67	317	32.3
AMERICAN STORES CO	12/31/67	332	26.1
AMETEK INC	12/31/67	1,476	31.2
BEMIS CO INC	12/31/67	558	28.5
BRUNSWICK CORP	12/31/67	171	37.2
GREAT LAKES CHEMICAL CORP	12/31/67	276	21.0
HARSCO CORP	12/31/67	122	37.0
HUBBELL INC -CL B	12/31/67	235	40.7
MASCO CORP	12/31/67	248	27.3
NUCOR CORP	12/31/67	1,813	24.5
PLDT-PHILIPPINE LNG DIST TEL	12/31/67	2,669	22.5
RUBBERMAID INC	12/31/67	159	24.2
U S BANCORP	12/31/67	986	29.0
WILLIAMS COS INC	12/31/67	252	32.5
MEDTRONIC PLC	10/31/68	969	24.7
PALL CORP	10/31/68	2,301	15.5
BESTFOODS	12/31/68	146	27.8
BOEING CO	12/31/68	987	19.8
BURLINGTON NORTHERN SANTA FE	12/31/68	419	27.0
CARLISLE COS INC	12/31/68	989	26.0
CSX CORP	12/31/68	391	36.0
GRAINGER (W W) INC	12/31/68	934	28.2
HONEYWELL INTERNATIONAL INC	12/31/68	177	41.8
ILLINOIS TOOL WORKS	12/31/68	848	28.0
MURPHY OIL CORP	12/31/68	281	33.0
NATIONAL FUEL GAS CO	12/31/68	388	30.5
NORFOLK SOUTHERN CORP	12/31/68	321	35.5
PPL CORP	12/31/68	147	36.5
ROCKWELL AUTOMATION	12/31/68	1,004	26.5
SANTA FE PACIFIC CORP	12/31/68	126	32.5
SONOCO PRODUCTS CO	12/31/68	335	27.5
MCCORMICK & CO INC	11/30/69	502	33.3
AMSOUTH BANCORPORATION	12/31/69	150	31.5

	Data Date	Total Return	Years to 100
LACLEDE GROUP INC	12/31/69	228	39.2
WAL-MART STORES INC	10/31/70	12,382	12.5
QUESTAR CORP	12/31/70	554	33.0
SYSCO CORP	12/31/70	1,249	21.5
TYCO INTERNATIONAL PLC	11/30/71	1,126	22.3
BCE INC	12/31/71	353	28.5
GENERAL DYNAMICS CORP	12/31/71	1,188	23.3
GRAHAM HOLDINGS CO	12/31/71	370	21.7
LOCKHEED MARTIN CORP	12/31/71	1,323	21.2
MEREDITH CORP	12/31/71	439	21.7
PITNEY BOWES INC	12/31/71	251	22.0
SOUTHWEST AIRLINES	12/31/71	5,478	9.5
BROWN-FORMAN -CL B	10/31/72	1,235	22.3
DONALDSON CO INC	10/31/72	643	26.3
LITTON INDUSTRIES INC	10/31/72	152	22.7
NORDSTROM INC	10/31/72	1,117	16.7
PVH CORP	10/31/72	460	19.3
SMUCKER (JM) CO	10/31/72	505	27.0
TARGET CORP	10/31/72	1,047	22.3
VALSPAR CORP	10/31/72	2,805	16.7
VORNADO REALTY TRUST	10/31/72	1,686	18.9
FAMILY DOLLAR STORES	11/30/72	3,987	10.2
HILL-ROM HOLDINGS INC	11/30/72	243	23.5
HONDA MOTOR CO LTD	11/30/72	108	33.8
LENNAR CORP	11/30/72	965	22.8
AETNA INC	12/31/72	222	31.0
AGL RESOURCES INC	12/31/72	316	29.3
ALBERTO-CULVER CO	12/31/72	730	21.5
ALLTEL CORP	12/31/72	200	24.3
AMERICAN GENERAL CORP	12/31/72	186	23.5
BALL CORP	12/31/72	843	28.2
BANK OF HAWAII CORP	12/31/72	300	28.3
BANK OF NEW YORK MELLON CORP	12/31/72	205	23.3
BANK ONE CORP	12/31/72	119	23.2
BP PLC	12/31/72	214	22.5

	Data Date	Total Return	Years to 100
CABOT CORP	12/31/72	334	23.5
CIGNA CORP	12/31/72	185	38.5
CLOROX CO/DE	12/31/72	536	23.0
COMMERCE BANCSHARES INC	12/31/72	266	27.2
CONAGRA FOODS INC	12/31/72	990	15.2
CONSOLIDATED EDISON INC	12/31/72	670	18.8
CURTISS-WRIGHT CORP	12/31/72	445	27.5
DOMINION RESOURCES INC	12/31/72	296	31.0
DTE ENERGY CO	12/31/72	223	36.2
DUKE ENERGY CORP	12/31/72	216	32.3
ELECTRONIC DATA SYSTEMS CORP	12/31/72	127	17.0
EVERSOURCE ENERGY	12/31/72	131	38.5
EXELON CORP	12/31/72	140	30.3
FLEETBOSTON FINANCIAL CORP	12/31/72	153	23.0
FLOWERS FOODS INC	12/31/72	1,706	22.2
FMC CORP	12/31/72	402	31.2
FOREST LABORATORIES -CL A	12/31/72	7,874	11.5
HARRIS CORP	12/31/72	274	31.0
HASBRO INC	12/31/72	3,725	9.5
HERSHEY CO	12/31/72	973	21.0
INTEL CORP	12/31/72	2,969	20.0
JOHNSON CONTROLS INC	12/31/72	991	22.3
KANSAS CITY SOUTHERN	12/31/72	16,931	18.2
LINCOLN NATIONAL CORP	12/31/72	111	32.0
MCGRAW HILL FINANCIAL	12/31/72	795	23.0
MCKESSON CORP	12/31/72	1,040	21.3
NEXTERA ENERGY INC	12/31/72	268	32.0
NSTAR	12/31/72	203	31.0
PARKER-HANNIFIN CORP	12/31/72	321	30.0
PROGRESS ENERGY INC	12/31/72	153	35.7
PUBLIC SERVICE ENTRP GRP INC	12/31/72	189	31.0
SAFECO CORP	12/31/72	134	30.7
SCANA CORP	12/31/72	199	33.3
SOUTHERN CO	12/31/72	329	27.5
STATE STREET CORP	12/31/72	1,490	17.3

	Data Date	Total Return	Years to 100
UGI CORP	12/31/72	395	30.3
VARIAN MEDICAL SYSTEMS INC	12/31/72	727	26.3
WALGREENS BOOTS ALLIANCE INC	12/31/72	2,161	16.9
WASTE MANAGEMENT INC-OLD	12/31/72	189	12.5
WGL HOLDINGS INC	12/31/72	234	32.0
ANALOG DEVICES	10/31/73	1,220	19.7
WILEY (JOHN) & SONS -CL A	10/31/73	929	22.0
BARNETT BANKS INC	12/31/73	122	22.0
EL PASO CGP CO	12/31/73	222	24.7
EQUIFAX INC	12/31/73	1,029	20.7
LANCASTER COLONY CORP	12/31/73	1,084	18.2
PACCAR INC	12/31/73	1,104	23.2
ALLEGHANY CORP	12/31/74	711	18.7
CANADIAN PACIFIC RAILWAY LTD	12/31/74	446	38.0
CHUBB CORP	12/31/74	265	31.3
LEGGETT & PLATT INC	12/31/74	924	18.2
M & T BANK CORP	12/31/74	827	19.8
PEPSIAMERICAS INC	12/31/74	126	30.5
EDWARDS (A G) INC	11/30/75	2,417	8.7
AMERICAN WATER WORKS INC	12/31/75	156	23.8
CBS CORP	12/31/75	630	14.7
DANAHER CORP	12/31/75	3,054	17.5
GOLDEN WEST FINANCIAL CORP	12/31/75	471	22.5
MCI COMMUNICATIONS	12/31/75	316	13.3
NOBLE ENERGY INC	12/31/75	185	32.0
UNION PACIFIC CORP	12/31/75	338	38.0
BRITISH AMER TOBACCO PLC	12/31/76	981	25.2
CHURCH & DWIGHT INC	12/31/76	447	28.3
SOUTHWESTERN ENERGY CO	12/31/77	160	28.5
GAP INC	10/31/78	1,666	11.0
L BRANDS INC	10/31/78	2,105	7.3
FEDEX CORP	11/30/78	154	35.5
AQUA AMERICA INC	12/31/79	137	31.5
CHRYSLER CORP	12/31/79	113	16.5
CONSTELLATION BRANDS	11/30/80	788	20.5

	Data Date	Total Return	Years to 100
APPLE INC	12/31/80	560	25.3
APPLIED MATERIALS INC	10/31/81	231	16.5
HOME DEPOT INC	10/31/81	3,172	9.7
RPM INTERNATIONAL INC	11/30/81	105	32.8
CA INC	12/31/81	160	13.8
COMCAST CORP	12/31/81	218	17.5
DOLLAR GENERAL CORP	12/31/81	196	15.8
ENBRIDGE INC	12/31/81	223	28.5
FRANKLIN ELECTRIC CO INC	12/31/81	147	30.3
FRANKLIN RESOURCES INC	12/31/81	11,363	4.2
GRACO INC	12/31/81	462	22.5
INTL GAME TECHNOLOGY	12/31/81	185	18.3
KLA-TENCOR CORP	12/31/81	141	18.0
MYLAN NV	12/31/81	803	11.5
PENTAIR PLC	12/31/81	125	31.3
PRECISION CASTPARTS CORP	12/31/81	653	22.8
ROBERT HALF INTL INC	12/31/81	528	15.7
SEI INVESTMENTS CO	12/31/81	256	19.8
SIGMA-ALDRICH CORP	12/31/81	171	31.5
STRYKER CORP	12/31/81	634	18.3
THERMO FISHER SCIENTIFIC INC	12/31/81	116	31.5
TYSON FOODS INC -CL A	12/31/81	176	31.2
EATON VANCE CORP	10/31/82	955	15.7
NORDSON CORP	10/31/82	140	28.7
NIKE INC	11/30/82	628	19.8
ROGERS COMMUNICATIONS -CL B	11/30/82	127	22.6
AFLAC INC	12/31/82	562	16.0
BBVA COMPASS BANCSHARES INC	12/31/82	209	21.8
BROOKFIELD ASSET MANAGEMENT	12/31/82	151	31.5
ENBRIDGE INC	12/31/82	254	28.5
SOUTHTRUST CORP	12/31/82	155	21.3
ST JUDE MEDICAL INC	12/31/82	399	17.0
TORCHMARK CORP	12/31/82	149	30.8
BIOMET INC	11/30/83	227	17.5
PAYCHEX INC	11/30/83	573	14.0

	Data Date	Total Return	Years to 100
AMGEN INC	12/31/83	1,632	10.7
CARDINAL HEALTH INC	12/31/83	119	29.2
IMMUNEX CORP	12/31/83	128	15.3
RAYMOND JAMES FINANCIAL CORP	12/31/83	297	21.0
TOTAL SYSTEM SERVICES INC	12/31/83	175	17.7
WILLIAMS-SONOMA INC	12/31/83	229	18.8
EXPEDITORS INTL WASH INC	12/31/84	337	16.5
RPC INC	12/31/84	152	24.3
AUTODESK INC	10/31/85	103	28.7
BEST BUY CO INC	12/31/85	271	13.7
JEFFERIES GROUP LLC	12/31/85	137	17.0
NOVO NORDISK A/S	12/31/85	289	22.5
PROGRESSIVE CORP-OHIO	12/31/85	118	28.0
UNITEDHEALTH GROUP INC	12/31/85	970	12.8
UNIVERSAL HEALTH SVCS INC	12/31/85	222	23.5
ADOBE SYSTEMS INC	11/30/86	391	13.5
ORACLE CORP	11/30/86	880	10.3
AIRGAS INC	12/31/86	128	26.2
FISERV INC	12/31/86	128	27.3
HARLEY-DAVIDSON INC	12/31/86	351	12.3
HEARTLAND EXPRESS INC	12/31/86	126	26.2
LINEAR TECHNOLOGY CORP	12/31/86	139	13.5
MICROSOFT CORP	12/31/86	680	10.8
PRICE (T. ROWE) GROUP	12/31/86	225	18.7
TEVA PHARMACEUTICALS	12/31/86	325	17.0
EMC CORP/MA	12/31/87	468	7.7
FASTENAL CO	12/31/87	382	17.0
HENRY (JACK) & ASSOCIATES	12/31/87	1,099	8.3
SCHWAB (CHARLES) CORP	12/31/87	299	11.0
DELL INC	10/31/88	270	7.2
ROSS STORES INC	10/31/88	395	19.5
ALTERA CORP	12/31/88	129	11.5
CERNER CORP	12/31/88	649	15.0
MAXIM INTEGRATED PRODUCTS	12/31/88	120	11.8
POLARIS INDUSTRIES INC	12/31/88	540	22.5

	Data Date	Total Return	Years to 100
MAGNA INTERNATIONAL INC	10/31/89	181	22.4
ELECTRONIC ARTS INC	12/31/89	104	14.0
CISCO SYSTEMS INC	10/31/90	353	7.3
AMPHENOL CORP	12/31/91	130	21.3
CANADIAN NATURAL RESOURCES	12/31/91	187	14.5
QUALCOMM INC	12/31/91	160	7.3
TOROMONT INDUSTRIES LTD	12/31/91	105	23.8
VECTOR GROUP LTD	12/31/91	370	8.5
ROPER INDUSTRIES INC/DE	10/31/92	117	21.4
BIOGEN IDEC INC	12/31/92	958	5.5
EXPRESS SCRIPTS HOLDING CO	12/31/92	425	13.5
GILEAD SCIENCES INC	12/31/92	355	18.3
NVR INC	12/31/92	232	9.7
REGENERON PHARMACEUTICALS	12/31/92	137	18.7
STARBUCKS CORP	12/31/92	127	21.3
TIME WARNER INC	12/31/92	488	6.0
CELGENE CORP	12/31/93	477	11.3
MONSTER BEVERAGE CORP	12/31/93	2,523	9.5
SVB FINANCIAL GROUP	12/31/93	174	25.2
VALEANT PHARMACEUTICALS INTL	12/31/94	815	6.5
ALEXION PHARMACEUTICALS INC	10/31/96	123	17.7
BP PRUDHOE BAY ROYALTY TRUST	12/31/96	141	11.7
KEURIG GREEN MOUNTAIN INC	12/31/96	722	10.7
AMAZON.COM INC	12/31/97	201	13.3
BALLY TECHNOLOGIES INC	12/31/98	132	13.3
TRACTOR SUPPLY CO	12/31/98	154	12.2
PRICELINE GROUP INC	12/31/99	145	12.5
ILLUMINA INC	12/31/01	163	11.0
QUESTCOR PHARMACEUTICALS INC	12/31/05	215	5.0
NEXSTAR BROADCASTING GROUP	12/31/06	105	5.0
PHARMACYCLICS INC	12/31/06	168	5.0

INDEX